QUESTIONS

VOLUME **8**

101 Outlandish and Amazing Q&As

Melina Gerosa Bellows

BRIGHT MATTER BOOKS

New York

Contents

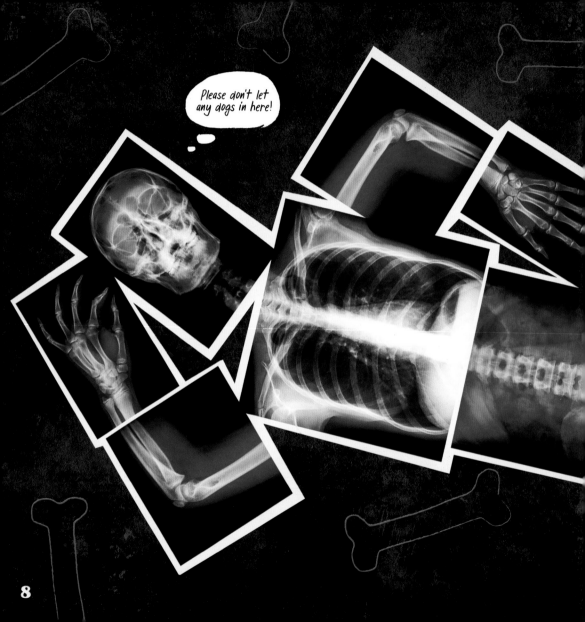

True or False:

Adults replace their skeleton every 10 years.

#1

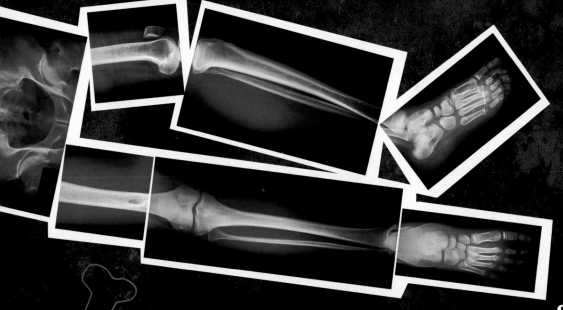

9

THE SKELETON COMPLETELY RENEWS ITSELF OVER THE COURSE OF 10 YEARS, thanks to hardworking cells that deconstruct and reconstruct different parts of the bone to keep the body healthy. The body's skeleton grows to its adult size in a process called modeling. But it doesn't stop there. **An adult skeleton slowly remodels,** or removes old bits of bone and replaces them with fresh bone tissue. **This keeps the bones strong and allows them to send calcium from food to the rest of body.** Calcium helps build and strengthen your bones as well as keeps all the cells in your body healthy.

Femur

Femur

Instant Genius

Femurs (thighbones) are the strongest bones in the human body.

Ca

What is **Baby Yinliang?**

a. a cartoon character

b. a miniature plant

c. a dinosaur fossil

a dinosaur fossil

BABY YINGLIANG, WHICH IS NAMED AFTER THE CHINESE MUSEUM WHERE IT LIVES, WAS A RARE AND LUCKY FIND. The 70-million-year-old fossil of an unhatched oviraptorid dinosaur is giving scientists clues to the connection between dinos and birds. Found in 2000, **the baby dinosaur inside the 7-inch (17-cm)-long egg was about 11 inches (28 cm) long** and would have grown to be 7 to 10 feet (2 to 3 m) long as an adult. Scientists from different countries teamed up to compare notes on Baby Yingliang and other oviraptorid embryo fossils. They found that the baby dino was "tucking," or moving and changing positions prior to hatching—**just like a baby bird would do before cracking free of its shell.** Talk about an egg-cellent discovery!

NOW YOU KNOW!
Oviraptors lived 75 million years ago, during the Cretaceous period. They could run as fast as an ostrich and could lay 20 eggs at a time.

Instant Genius
Oviraptor means "egg thief."

Why doesn't gum dissolve?

#3

a. because it doesn't break down in water

b. because of the flavoring

c. It does if you keep chewing it.

13

NEARLY ALL GUM CONTAINS A COMBINATION OF THREE THINGS: RESIN, WAX, AND A SUBSTANCE CALLED ELASTOMER. The resin makes up the bulk of the gum, while the wax and elastomer keep it soft and chewy. **Resin often contains a synthetic, or man-made, substance.** Sometimes the same stuff is used to make plastic bottles and bags. Other times it's the stuff used in car tires or latex paints. **These synthetic materials are what keeps gum from disintegrating when you chew it.** These rubbers are not water soluble, and therefore do not dissolve in saliva, like food does. **Some don't even dissolve in stomach acid.** But don't worry—chewing gum is usually considered safe, and if you accidently swallow a piece, you will pass it whole when you go to the bathroom.

Instant Genius

Some chemists are paid to create gum flavors and make them last longer.

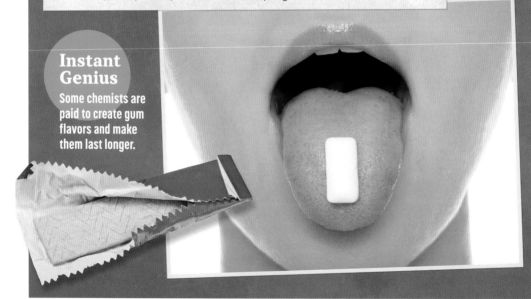

#4

True or False:

All birds have the same number of feathers.

15

ANSWER: False

BIRDS ARE THE ONLY ANIMALS WITH FEATHERS, AND EVERY BIRD HAS THEM. However, not all birds have the same number. **Hummingbirds have the fewest at about 1,000.** The bigger the bird, the more feathers it might have. The emperor penguin has a dense coat of feathers with 100 per square inch, for a total of about 80,000 feathers. **Not all feathers serve the same purpose. Brightly colored peacock feathers, for instance, are meant to attract mates.** And flight feathers, which are particularly solid and tough, grow on the wings of birds to help them stay in the air when flying. **Feathers also function to keep birds warm,** protect them from the elements, camouflage them from predators, and help birds that swim to maneuver in the water and dive below the surface to catch prey.

NOW YOU KNOW!
To help them keep warm, birds who live in colder climates have more fluffy down on their feathers than other birds.

Instant Genius
Male sandgrouses carry water in their belly feathers.

16

What gives Mosquito Bay its blue light?

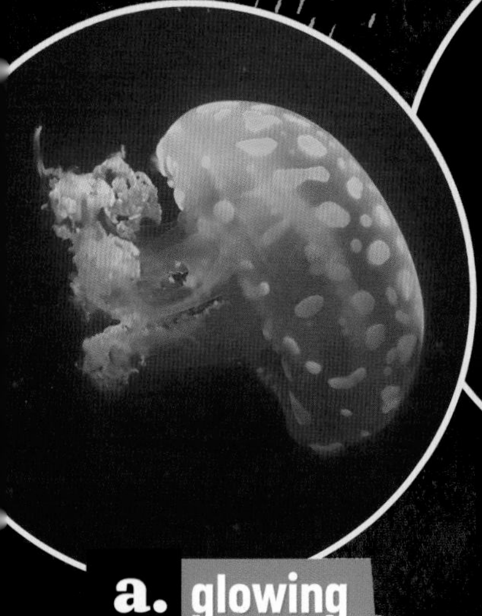

a. glowing organisms

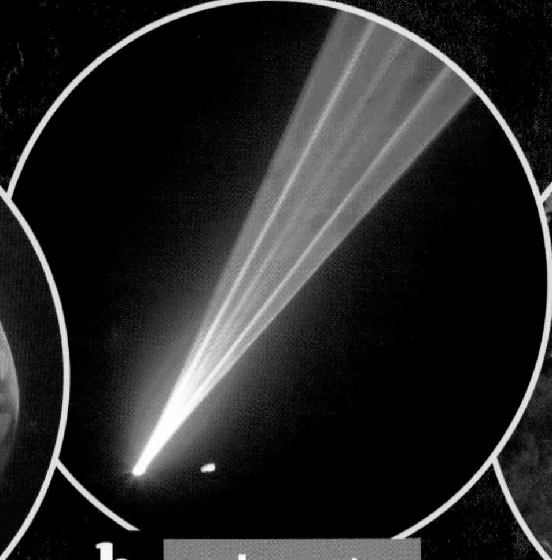

b. underwater lasers

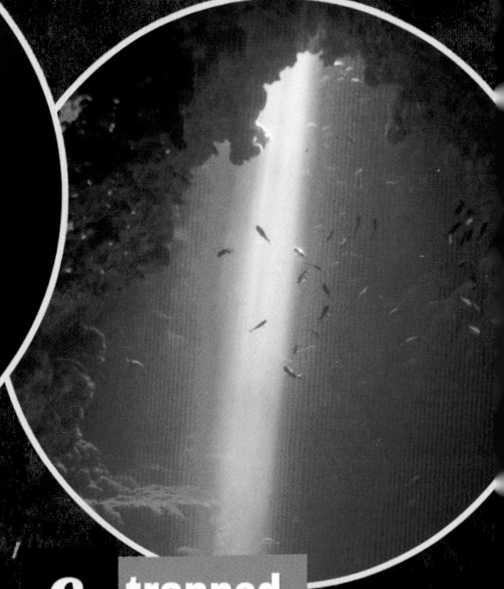

c. trapped sunlight

glowing organisms

ON THE SOUTH SIDE OF THE PUERTO RICAN ISLAND OF VIEQUES, YOU'LL FIND AN EERIE NIGHTTIME SIGHT—a blue glow coming from the water! **Tiny organisms called dinoflagellates make the illumination.** These tiny sea creatures convert their internal chemical energy into a natural light called bioluminescence. **These microscopic creatures produce light 100 times larger than their teeny bodies.** Every time they detect movement in the water, they shoot out blue-green streaks, illuminating areas of the bay like underwater lightning.

Instant Genius

Some fish, worms, and crustaceans can produce bioluminescence, too.

Why was the internet invented?

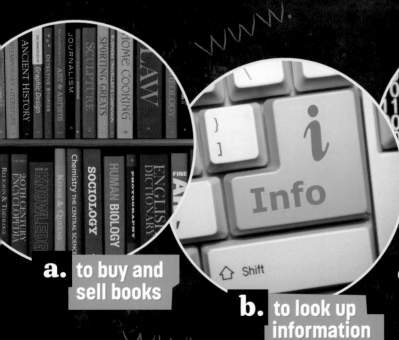

a. to buy and sell books

b. to look up information

c. to be used as a spy tool

to be used as a spy tool

THE WORLD WIDE WEB MAY HAVE BEEN INTRODUCED IN 1989, but a version of the internet originated decades earlier. In the 1950s, during a period called the Cold War, tensions between the United States and the Soviet Union were at an all-time high. Each side wanted access to information about the other. **The United States needed a secure system for sending and receiving important information,** and they turned to large computers called supercomputers. But supercomputers were expensive, extremely heavy, and difficult to access. **In the mid-1960s, researchers in the United States developed a computer network that only certain scientists, military personnel, and university staff could access.** By the late 1970s, the technology had developed so that **the general public could have computers in their homes and offices.**

An operator sits at the control board of PENNSTAC (Penn State Automatic Computer), State College, Pennsylvania, 1964.

NOW YOU KNOW!
The "www" that you often see at the start of a URL stands for World Wide Web.

Instant Genius
About 60 percent of internet use happens on mobile devices.

Apple III personal computer, 1980

True or False:

Sharkskin
is always smooth.

#7

Instant Genius

Underwater, a shark's vision is about 10 times better than a human's.

ANSWER: **False**

SHARKSKIN CAN BE SMOOTH OR ROUGH, DEPENDING ON HOW YOU TOUCH IT. How? Sharkskin is made of small, teethlike scales, called dermal denticles. These scales help the shark swim faster by reducing friction and turbulence from the water. **The "teeth" face toward the tail,** so if you were to run your hand along the shark from its head to its tail, the skin would feel soft and smooth. **From the other direction, however, the sharp, little denticles would feel rough, like sandpaper.** The scales help the shark fend off parasites and predators. The denticles also make for quiet swimming. **Some swimwear designers have taken note and added fake sharkskin to their swimsuits.** These special suits copy the exact proportions of the scales to help athletes swim faster.

A swimmer wearing a fake sharkskin swimsuit

How many **breaths** do you take **each day?**

a. 250

b. 2,500

c. 25,000

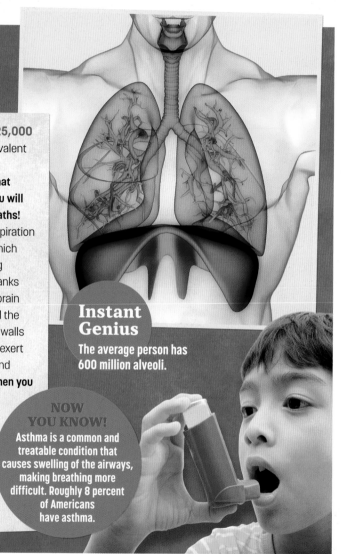

25,000

HUMAN BEINGS TAKE ABOUT 25,000 BREATHS PER DAY! That's equivalent to roughly 16 breaths per minute, or 8.4 million breaths per year. **That means, by the time you're 80, you will have taken about 500 billion breaths!** Children have an even higher respiration rate of 44 breaths per minute, which slows down as we age. Breathing itself is automatic. It happens thanks to neurons in a deep part of the brain called the brain stem that control the muscle groups that make up the walls of your respiratory system. They exert force, contracting the muscles and moving air through your body. **When you breathe in, the air goes into your lungs, where you have tiny sacs called alveoli.** The alveoli are surrounded by blood vessels, called capillaries, which pass oxygen into your blood and transport it into your bloodstream and to your heart.

Instant Genius

The average person has 600 million alveoli.

NOW YOU KNOW!

Asthma is a common and treatable condition that causes swelling of the airways, making breathing more difficult. Roughly 8 percent of Americans have asthma.

How long is a day on
Pluto?

a. **6.4 Earth hours**

b. **6.4 Earth days**

c. **6.4 Earth years**

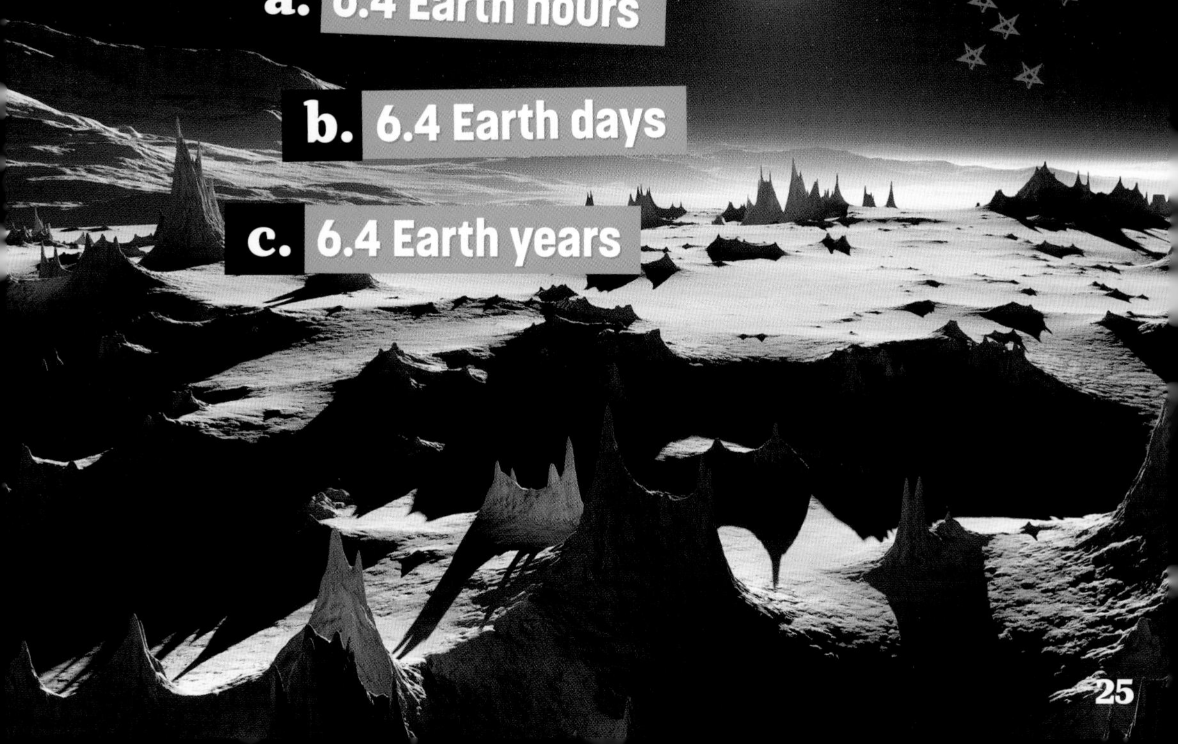

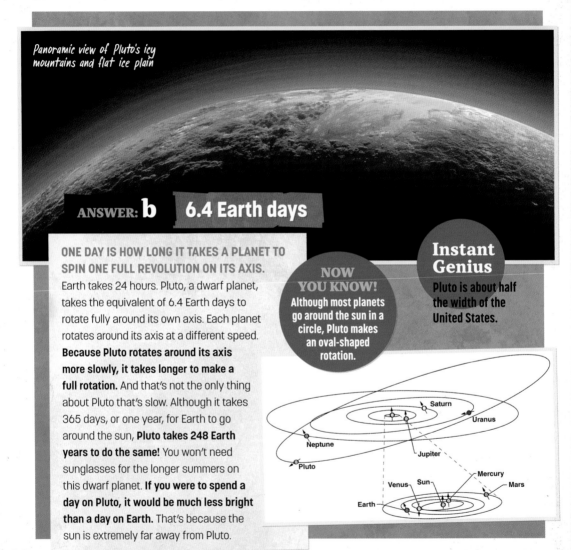

Panoramic view of Pluto's icy mountains and flat ice plain

ANSWER: b | **6.4 Earth days**

ONE DAY IS HOW LONG IT TAKES A PLANET TO SPIN ONE FULL REVOLUTION ON ITS AXIS. Earth takes 24 hours. Pluto, a dwarf planet, takes the equivalent of 6.4 Earth days to rotate fully around its own axis. Each planet rotates around its axis at a different speed. **Because Pluto rotates around its axis more slowly, it takes longer to make a full rotation.** And that's not the only thing about Pluto that's slow. Although it takes 365 days, or one year, for Earth to go around the sun, **Pluto takes 248 Earth years to do the same!** You won't need sunglasses for the longer summers on this dwarf planet. **If you were to spend a day on Pluto, it would be much less bright than a day on Earth.** That's because the sun is extremely far away from Pluto.

NOW YOU KNOW!
Although most planets go around the sun in a circle, Pluto makes an oval-shaped rotation.

Instant Genius
Pluto is about half the width of the United States.

Saturn

Uranus

Neptune

Jupiter

Pluto

Venus

Sun

Mercury

Mars

Earth

26

How big
was the
world's largest
arthropod?

a. the size of a dinner plate

b. the size of a golden retriever

c. the size of a car

ANSWER: C **the size of a car**

IF TODAY'S MILLIPEDES GIVE YOU THE CREEPS, imagine a millipede as big as a car! That's just what scientists believe was discovered in northern England in 2018. They estimate that the fossil fragment found inside a chunk of sandstone represents an **8.6-foot (2.6-m)-long, 110-pound (50-kg) invertebrate** that dates back about 326 million years. That means that **100 million years before dinosaurs existed, gigantic arthropods roamed Earth!**

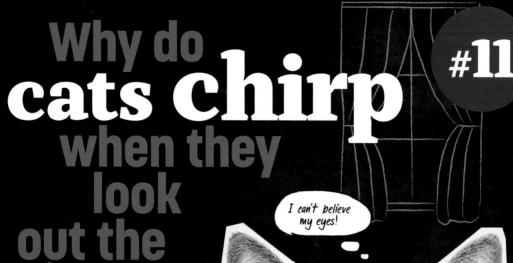

Why do cats chirp when they look out the window?

a. They're bored.

b. They see prey.

c. They want your attention.

ANSWER: b **They see prey.**

THE NEXT TIME YOU NOTICE YOUR KITTY MAKING STRANGE NOISES AT THE WINDOW, it's likely just her predatory instincts kicking in. When a cat sees a bird, rodent, or insect and gets excited, **it produces a sound known as chattering.** Also known as chirping or twittering, chattering is basically your cat's way of saying **"Wow! Check it out!"** A kitty's ears tilted forward and eyes widened are further signs that **her whole body is on high alert and laser-focused on what she's seeing out there.**

Instant Genius

A group of kittens is called a kindle.

True or False: Some dogs can detect cancer.

#12

31

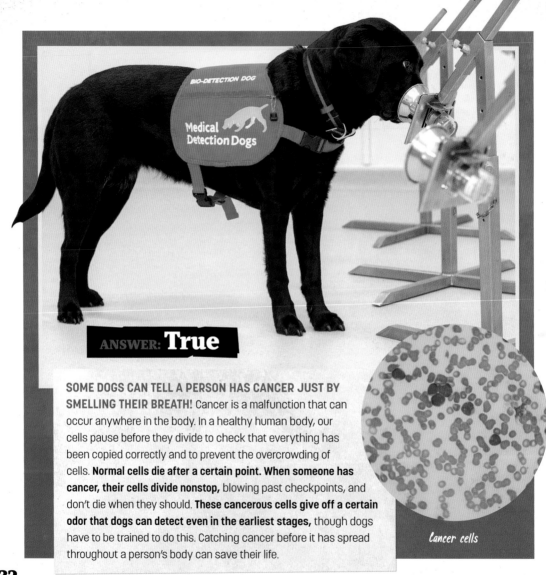

ANSWER: **True**

SOME DOGS CAN TELL A PERSON HAS CANCER JUST BY SMELLING THEIR BREATH! Cancer is a malfunction that can occur anywhere in the body. In a healthy human body, our cells pause before they divide to check that everything has been copied correctly and to prevent the overcrowding of cells. **Normal cells die after a certain point. When someone has cancer, their cells divide nonstop,** blowing past checkpoints, and don't die when they should. **These cancerous cells give off a certain odor that dogs can detect even in the earliest stages,** though dogs have to be trained to do this. Catching cancer before it has spread throughout a person's body can save their life.

Cancer cells

How long does it take plastic to break down in the ocean?

a. 45 days b. 45 years c. 450 years

Plastic pollution on a beach in Bali, Indonesia

NOW YOU KNOW!

Plastic production is set to double by the year 2050, and each year 8 million tons (7 million t) more plastic waste pollutes the ocean.

ANSWER: C

450 years

ACCORDING TO THE NATIONAL OCEANIC AND ATMOSPHERIC ADMINISTRATION, plastic only degrades—or breaks down—after 450 years. But a recent scientific advancement, a chemical mixture called a "super enzyme," can speed up the degradation process. **This is an exciting invention because it might allow people to recycle plastic more quickly.** The "super enzyme" would make a big impact because currently 359 million tons (320 million t) of plastic are made on Earth every year—and more than 150 million tons (134 million t) of waste plastic are left to decompose. **Plastic pollution is one of the greatest challenges scientists face in working to address global climate change.**

Instant Genius

Half of all plastics in the world were produced in the last 15 years.

#14

Serena Williams bounces a tennis ball five times before each first serve.

SERENA WILLIAMS IS ONE OF THE GREATEST TENNIS PLAYERS OF ALL TIME. Both Serena and her sister, Venus, got their start at the public tennis courts in Los Angeles and went on to be tennis stars and Olympic gold medalists. **Like many athletes, Serena is known to be incredibly superstitious.** This means that she has a belief not based in fact. For example, during every match, she bounces her tennis ball five times before each first serve for good luck. **And if she's having a winning streak, she will wear the same pair of socks throughout the whole competition.** But whether from the ball bouncing or her punishing training regimen, with 4 Olympic gold medals and 39 total Grand Slam triumphs under her belt, Serena is clearly making it work!

NOW YOU KNOW!
Serena started playing tennis when she was just three years old.

Instant Genius
Other than tennis, Serena's favorite sport to watch is gymnastics.

How do some Japanese water beetles survive being **swallowed** by a frog?

They call me Big Gulp.

a. They hold their breath.

b. They make the frog poop.

c. They turn into poison.

Enochrus japonicus

ANSWER: **b**

They make the frog poop.

SCIENTISTS WERE SURPRISED TO FIND THAT ONE SPECIES OF JAPANESE WATER BEETLE CAN SURVIVE THE ACIDIC DIGESTIVE TRACT OF A FROG—when they saw one pop out of a frog's poop alive! Studies have shown that **the beetle uses its hind legs to push through the frog's inches-long digestive system,** which, for a little beetle, is quite a stretch. The beetle's strong exoskeleton protects the bug from the frog's stomach acid, and **its sleek shape allows for it to speedily travel through the frog's digestive tract.** When the beetle finally reaches the end of the frog's digestive system, **it contracts and releases muscles in its hind legs to tickle the frog.** Eventually the frog excretes the beetle along with its poop. Talk about an exit strategy!

NOW YOU KNOW!
Other species are known to travel through digestive tracts too. Killifish eggs can survive the digestive systems of swans.

What is the terminator line?

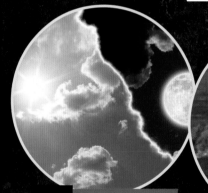

a. a line that separates day from night

b. the very edge of a cliff

c. the last day of a report card's marking period

a line that separates day from night

A LITERAL LINE, CALLED THE TERMINATOR LINE, SEPARATES NIGHT AND DAY. From space, it appears fuzzy because of our atmosphere. On Earth, we experience the line as dawn and dusk. **When we see the sun rising and setting, we are the ones actually moving, not the sun.** It takes 24 hours for Earth to revolve once around its axis, which makes a day. When the sun rises, Earth is turning toward the sun, and when it sets, Earth is turning away from it. **Although we see one sunrise and sunset every 24 hours, astronauts on the International Space Station see multiple around the world,** because their spacecraft speeds around Earth every 92 minutes. However, the spacecraft is moving so fast that each one only lasts a couple seconds!

Terminator line

Daytime

Nighttime

Instant Genius

The East Cape in New Zealand sees the sunrise first, before other parts of the world.

True or False:

All of your fingers have
three joints.

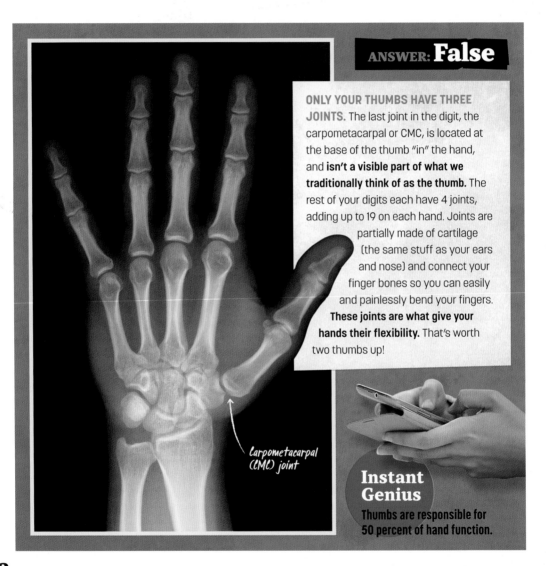

ONLY YOUR THUMBS HAVE THREE JOINTS. The last joint in the digit, the carpometacarpal or CMC, is located at the base of the thumb "in" the hand, and **isn't a visible part of what we traditionally think of as the thumb.** The rest of your digits each have 4 joints, adding up to 19 on each hand. Joints are partially made of cartilage (the same stuff as your ears and nose) and connect your finger bones so you can easily and painlessly bend your fingers. **These joints are what give your hands their flexibility.** That's worth two thumbs up!

Carpometacarpal (CMC) joint

Instant Genius

Thumbs are responsible for 50 percent of hand function.

What are your chances of finding a four-leaf clover?

#18

a. one in 100

b. one in 10,000

c. one in one million

FOUR-LEAF CLOVERS ARE INCREDIBLY RARE because they are a genetic mutation of their more common counterparts, three-leaf clovers. Finding a four-leaf clover is a one in 10,000 chance, and finding two in a row is nearly impossible. **Each leaf on the clover is said to stand for a certain trait: faith, hope, love, and—of course—luck.** If you do find one of these rare charms, legend says that good luck will come your way, but only if the clover is found by accident. **This superstition started with Celtic priests in Ireland, who always carried three-leaf and four-leaf clovers with them to ward off evil spirits.** In the Middle Ages, children thought that if they kept a clover with them, they could see fairies.

NOW YOU KNOW!
A woman in Glen Alpine, a suburb of Sydney, Australia, once found a clover patch with 21 four-leaf clovers in it.

St. PATRICK.

True or False:

Spiders are insects.

#19

Most spiders eat other spiders.

A black widow spider wrapping a grasshopper

ANSWER: **False**

NOW YOU KNOW!
Scorpions, ticks, mites, and pseudoscorpions (scorpions without a stinger) are also arachnids.

INSECTS ONLY HAVE SIX LEGS. SPIDERS—PART OF A GROUP OF BUGS KNOWN AS ARACHNIDS—HAVE EIGHT LEGS, along with an abdomen and a cephalothorax (a combined head and midsection). These eight-legged bugs aren't insects, but they sure do like to eat them! **Insects make up the majority of these carnivores' diets, but bigger spiders can eat fish, frogs, snakes, and even birds.** Some spiders strike and paralyze their prey with venom-packed fangs before wrapping them up in thick webs to save their snack for later. **Altogether, there are more than 45,000 spider species.** Most spiders are harmless, but beware of others. The black widow spider, for example, is extremely poisonous to humans.

What did **Sir Isaac Newton** discover?

a. locomotion

b. the law of gravity

c. electricity

the law of gravity

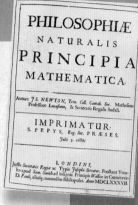

ONE OF THE MOST INFLUENTIAL SCIENTISTS OF ALL TIME, ISAAC NEWTON DISCOVERED THAT GRAVITY IS UNIVERSAL. This means that the force that causes a ball to fall to the ground after it is thrown is the same force that holds Earth and the other planets in orbit around the sun. **Newton published the theory of universal gravitation in his groundbreaking book *Principia*,** in which he also established the three laws of motion, forming the foundation of modern physics. After the book was published in 1687, **Newton became a very important member of British society, later becoming Sir Isaac Newton, when Queen Anne of England knighted him.** Newton also studied subjects such as chemistry and optics, which refers to how we see things. He discovered, for example, that white light is actually made up of many different colors.

Sir Isaac Newton featured on the Bank of England's one-pound note between 1978 and 1988.

Sir Isaac Newton 1642–1727

NOW YOU KNOW!
For nearly three decades, Sir Isaac Newton was also the Master of the Mint, responsible for all of England's currency, or money.

Which country makes most of the world's robots?

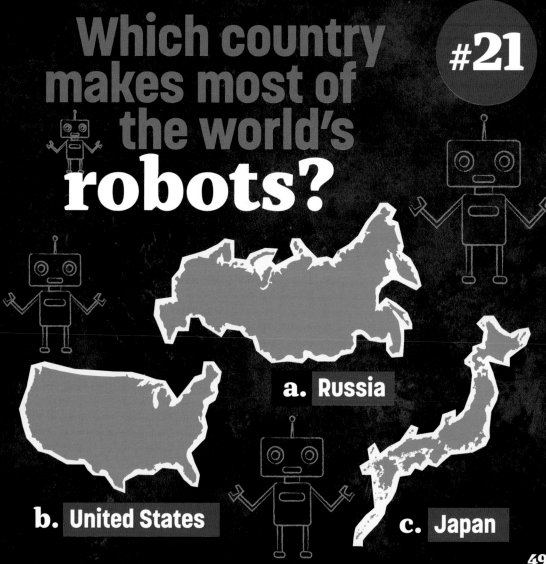

a. Russia

b. United States

c. Japan

21

Japan

JAPAN IS THE WORLD LEADER IN ROBOT MANUFACTURING, building roughly **45 percent of the world's supply of robots.** Their robot makers' technical abilities were on full display at the 2020 Olympic Games in Tokyo. Robots at the event were developed to greet guests, show them to their seats, serve food, and retrieve sporting equipment. **Outside the arena, Tokyo is a futuristic city in many ways.** People in the city enjoy many forms of advanced technology here, including **superfast bullet trains, teeny capsule hotels, luxuriously heated toilets, and even robot-operated restaurants.**

NOW YOU KNOW!
Some high-tech toilets are self-cleaning, and can check your weight and blood pressure while you sit.

True or False:

Your skin is mostly water.

MADE OF 64 PERCENT WATER, SKIN IS THE BODY'S LARGEST ORGAN, AND ALSO THE HEAVIEST. Altogether, skin makes up about one-seventh of the body's total weight and covers a surface area of about 16 to 22 square feet (1.5–2 sq m). **Your skin has three layers—the outermost layer is the epidermis, followed by the dermis, then the subcutis.** Inside the subcutis layer are tiny cavities filled with fat and water. **The water in your skin serves as a moisturizer that keeps the skin healthy and flexible.** The fat acts as a shock absorber that protects internal organs and bones from getting damaged in accidents. **To keep your skin healthy and body functioning, drink two liters or about eight cups of water a day,** in addition to the water you get from food you eat.

Epidermis

Dermis

Subcutis

Instant Genius

You can only survive about three days without water.

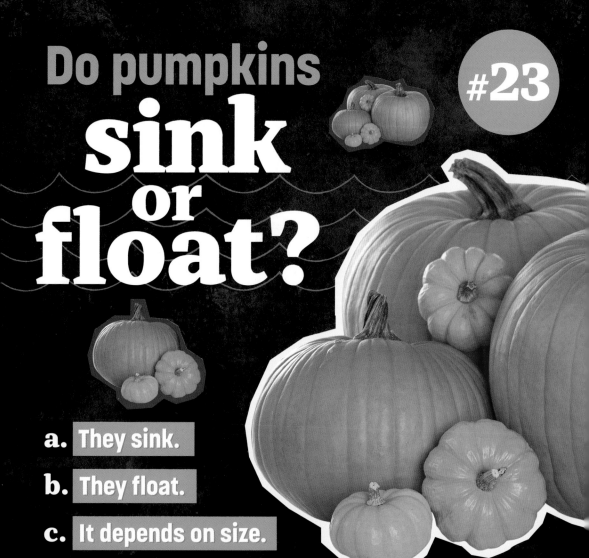

Do pumpkins sink or float?

#23

a. They sink.

b. They float.

c. It depends on size.

ANSWER: b **They float.**

PUMPKINS ARE LESS DENSE THAN WATER, SO THEY FLOAT. That means that, if you had a container filled with water, it would weigh more than the same container filled with pumpkins. **We have the ancient Greek scientist and thinker Archimedes to thank for explaining how density works.** According to legend, he was tasked with proving whether or not a king's crown was made of pure gold. At first, Archimedes was stumped. **Then an idea struck while he was taking a bath.** Water overflowed from the tub when he got in. The scientist realized the amount of displaced water could help him figure out an object's weight, which could hold clues about the materials that made it. **Archimedes supposedly leaped from his bathtub and ran into the streets shouting "Eureka!" when he figured it out!**

Which animal travels the farthest?

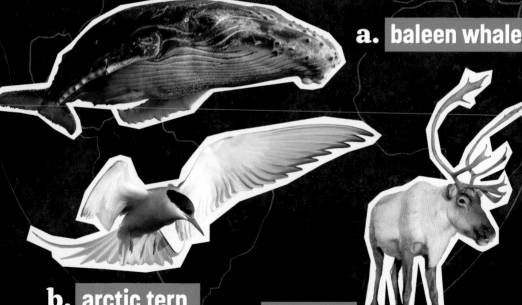

a. baleen whale

b. arctic tern

c. caribou

ANSWER: b

arctic tern

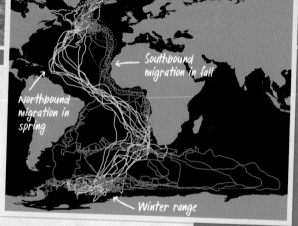

Southbound migration in fall

Northbound migration in spring

Winter range

ANIMALS MIGRATE, OR TRAVEL FROM ONE REGION TO ANOTHER, TO WARMER LOCATIONS WHERE THEY CAN FIND FOOD AND MATE. Scientists discovered that the arctic tern makes the longest recorded migration of any known animal. **This migration takes place yearly between Greenland and Antarctica along a route that's approximately 44,000 miles (70,800 km) long.** In their lifetime, this adds up to about 1.5 million miles (2.4 million km) of travel. To measure the birds' distance and track their patterns of movement, **scientists attached a small, lightweight tracking device to the birds' legs.** They found that arctic terns don't migrate in a direct line. Instead, they fly in a zigzag pattern, stopping in Africa and South America, as they follow the wind.

Tracking device, actual size

True or False:

All ancient Egyptians were

mummified.

Where's my mummy?

ANSWER: **False**

MUMMIFICATION WAS VERY EXPENSIVE, AND NOT MANY PEOPLE COULD AFFORD IT. Most pharaohs were mummified. People born into a high class or rank and powerful people who worked in the government were also often mummified, and anyone else who had the money could be, too. Most common people, however, could not go through the mummification process. **Common Egyptians were most likely wrapped in a simple cloth and buried in the desert** with a bit of food and some favorite objects to take with them to the afterlife. **Sometimes, for religious reasons, animals were also mummified. Sacred bulls in one village even had their own cemetery.**

Instant Genius

Egyptians believed the mummified body was the home for the soul.

How big is a #26 cat's brain?

a. the size of a pea

b. the size of a walnut

c. the size of a plum

ANSWER: b

the size of a walnut

A CAT'S BRAIN MAY SEEM SMALL AT ONLY THE SIZE OF A WALNUT, BUT IT'S PACKED WITH AROUND 300 MILLION NEURONS. Most of the action happens in an area of the brain called the cerebral cortex. Just like in your brain, **the cerebral cortex is the section responsible for making decisions and solving problems.** It is also where short-term and long-term memories are stored. **Scientists think this brain activity could explain why cats are more independent than other types of domesticated animals.** In one study, researchers had cats and dogs solve a puzzle to get treats. The cats independently tried to solve the puzzle until they got it right. **The dogs, on the other hand, consistently looked to the humans to help them figure it out.**

Want a tip?

About how many **Earths** could fit in the **sun?**

a. 100   **b.** 1 million   **c.** 10 trillion

ANSWER: b **1 million**

THE SUN IS SO BIG THAT IT COULD FIT ABOUT 1.3 MILLION EARTHS INSIDE IT. In fact, Earth is so small in comparison that it's only about as large as the average sunspot. **The sun, on the other hand, is about 864,400 miles (1.4 million km) in diameter.** The average temperature there is a sizzling 10,000 °F (5500 °C) on the surface, and 27,000,000 °F (15,000,000 °C) at the core. But the sun in our solar system is not even the biggest or the hottest star in the universe. **Astronomers have discovered stars that are 100 times bigger than the sun,** and also stars that are 12 times hotter than the sun!

Where can you see #28
pink
dolphins?

a. Mexico

b. Australia

c. Brazil

Brazil

NOW YOU KNOW!
The goliath birdeater tarantula, blue morpho butterfly, and basilisk lizard are all species also found in the Amazon rainforest.

AMAZON RIVER DOLPHINS, ALSO KNOWN AS PINK DOLPHINS OR BOTOS, are an endangered species found in the Amazon and Orinoco River basins of South America. Despite their name, they are not all pink. **The dolphins are born gray, and only the males turn pink with age.** Scientists think that the pink is scar tissue from fighting or rough play. **Amazon River dolphins can only survive in freshwater,** and their diet mainly consists of fish and crustaceans. These dolphins can bend at an impressive 90-degree angle to bob and weave through the dense underwater roots of the rainforest river.

Which baseball player has hit the **most** home runs?

a. Barry Bonds

b. Alex Rodriguez

c. Sammy Sosa

#29

65

Barry Bonds

BARRY BONDS, ONE OF THE MOST SUCCESSFUL MAJOR LEAGUE BASEBALL (MLB) PLAYERS OF ALL TIME, holds the world record for the most career home runs: a remarkable 762! **Bonds played as an outfielder for the Pittsburgh Pirates from 1986 to 1992 and for the San Francisco Giants from 1993 to 2007.** After college, he was drafted first by the Pirates, then went on to break the MLB's records for most career home runs, most home runs in a season, and most career walks. **His single-season best was set in 2001, when he hit 73 total home runs** while with the San Francisco Giants. Because of his success, **Barry Bonds has received 8 Gold Glove Awards, 7 National League MPV Awards, and 14 All-Star selections.**

Instant Genius

Barry Bonds stole 514 bases in his professional career.

True or False:

#30

The computer Alexa stores everything you ever tell it.

ALEXA, AMAZON'S DIGITAL ASSISTANT, CAN USE ARTIFICIAL INTELLIGENCE TO ANSWER ALMOST ANY QUESTION YOU ASK HER and can perform many simple tasks. But be careful with your questions, because Alexa will remember everything you say. **Once activated, Alexa records the interaction from start to finish,** then stores the conversation onto a cloud drive Amazon owns. Most of the time, no one ever hears it. But in at least two cases, in Arkansas and Florida, **police have requested recordings to help investigate crimes.** However, no evidence was found on the Alexa device.

What are fossils made of?

b. rock

a. ancient bones

c. hair and skin

ANSWER: b rock

THE WORD *FOSSIL* COMES FROM THE LATIN WORD *FOSSUS*, WHICH MEANS "HAVING BEEN DUG UP." Fossils are the preserved remains of ancient organisms often found in rock layers very deep inside Earth. **For an organism to become a fossil, it needs to be covered with sediment**—such as mud, ash, or sand—soon after its death. Over time, the sediment seeps into the remains, which are usually hard parts like shells or bones, to take the shape of the organism. **So, fossils are not the bones of an organism, but newly shaped rock.** Fossils are important to paleontologists because they give clues about where the organisms lived and what their environment was like in the prehistoric past.

How long can the gastrointestinal tract be?

a. up to 9 inches (23 cm)

b. up to 2 feet (0.6 m)

c. up to 30 feet (9 m)

ANSWER: C — **up to 30 feet (9 m)**

THE GASTROINTESTINAL TRACT, OR GI TRACT FOR SHORT, IS A SERIES OF DIGESTIVE ORGANS UP TO 30 FEET (9 M) LONG. It starts with your mouth and continues down to your esophagus, stomach, to the small and large intestines. **The GI tract is responsible for swallowing and digesting food.** After you swallow, your GI tract moves food through the body by a process called peristalsis. The walls surrounding your esophagus move together to **push the food like an internal wave from the top of your throat to the pit of your stomach.** Then the stomach dissolves the food with highly corrosive acid. Whatever waste remains eventually moves out of your body and into the toilet. **The whole process from start to finish can take anywhere from 6 hours to several days!**

NOW YOU KNOW!
Your body can move food through your digestive system even while you're standing on your head.

True or False:

#33

Driving at high speed, it would take about two months to circle Saturn's rings.

Instant Genius

The Cassini spacecraft was destroyed in Saturn's atmosphere in 2017.

ANSWER: **False**

IF YOU WERE DRIVING 75 MILES (121 KM) AN HOUR, IT WOULD TAKE 258 DAYS, or about nine months, to complete a lap of Saturn's rings. Saturn is the second largest planet in our solar system, after Jupiter. Without its rings, Saturn is as wide as nine Earths side by side. **The planet's seven large rings reach 175,000 miles (282,000 km) away from the planet's surface** and have a height of 30 feet (9 m). They're made up of comets, asteroids, and other rock forms broken apart by Saturn's powerful gravity. **These chunks of rock and ice range in size from a grain of salt to the heft of a mountain!**

NOW YOU KNOW!

Saturn's large rings are made up of smaller rings, sometimes called ringlets.

How did
Susan B. Anthony
change women's rights?

#34

a. She helped women get the right to vote.

b. She helped women enlist in the war effort.

c. She invented coins.

She helped women get the right to vote.

SUFFRAGISTS WERE WOMEN IN THE EARLY 1900s WHO FOUGHT FOR WOMEN'S RIGHT TO VOTE AND TO BE SEEN AS EQUALS TO MEN. Susan B. Anthony, who led the suffragist charge for more than 50 years, was one of the most important suffragists in history. Born into a Quaker family in 1820, **Anthony was driven by her teachings that all people were created equal.** Anthony worked hard for many years, and allied with people like journalist William Lloyd Garrison and statesman Frederick Douglass to **end slavery and give all Americans the right to vote.** She gave speeches, wrote petitions, led protests, and nearly got arrested countless times, but she never gave up. Eventually, Anthony's hard work paid off with **passing of the 19th Amendment in 1920, granting women in the United States the right to vote.**

Instant Genius

Susan B. Anthony died in 1906, 14 years before women got the right to vote.

NOW YOU KNOW!

The Susan B. Anthony U.S. dollar coin was minted from 1979 to 1981 and again in 1999. It was the first time a woman was featured on a U.S. coin.

#35

How big is the eye of a hurricane?

a. 20–40 feet (6–12 m)

b. 2–4 miles (3.2–6.4 km)

c. 20–40 miles (32–64 km)

KS AND
ICOS

An infrared satellite photo of Hurricane Irma, 2017

DOMINICAN REPUBLIC

PUERTO RICO

ANSWER: **C**

20–40 miles (32–64 km)

HURRICANES ARE LARGE STORMS WITH WIND SPEED OF HIGHER THAN 74 MILES (119 KM) AN HOUR. The center of the rotating storm is called the eye. Eyes of hurricanes are generally round and can be between 20 and 30 miles (32 and 48 km) wide. **However, unlike the chaotic storm swirling around it, the eye is calm.** Inside, air pressure is low, the sky is clear, and winds are light. **The eye of a storm is shaped like a cylinder and extends down through the clouds like a chimney.** Surrounding it is the eye wall, which is the most dangerous part of the storm because the wind is the strongest there. Eye walls are made up of **towering thunderstorms with wind speeds that can whip up to 155 miles (249 km) an hour.**

Instant Genius

Cumulonimbus clouds cause heavy rain, hail, snow, lightning, and tornadoes.

True or False:

#36

Beaver urine

is sometimes used in vanilla flavoring.

Instant Genius
Beavers can see underwater.

ANSWER: **True**

NOW YOU KNOW!
The scientific name for the beaver is *Castor canadensis*. There are two types of beaver: the Eurasian and the North American.

BEAVERS MARK THEIR TERRITORY BY PEEING A SPECIAL CHEMICAL CALLED CASTOREUM. It's produced in castor glands near the base of their tails, and **it's not uncommon for the beaver's urine to, um, mix in with the chemical.** This sweet-scented chemical has been used in perfumes and food flavoring for more than 90 years. **People actually milk beavers to get it!** But don't worry: It's safe to eat and wear. Some high-fashion brands even use it in their scents.

Which U.S. city has the largest surface area?

a. New York, New York

b. Los Angeles, California

c. Sitka, Alaska

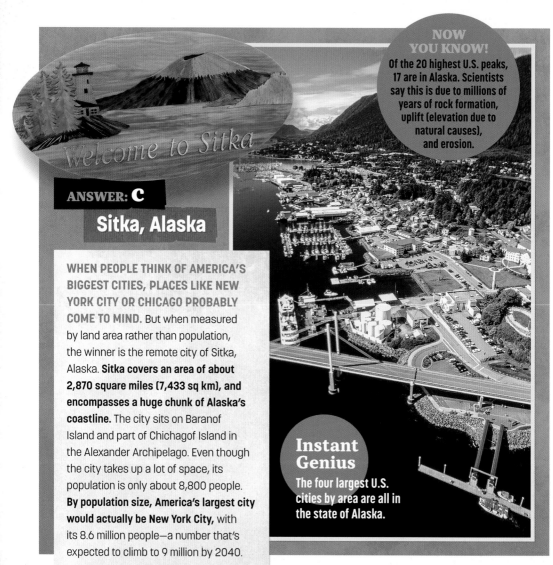

NOW YOU KNOW!

Of the 20 highest U.S. peaks, 17 are in Alaska. Scientists say this is due to millions of years of rock formation, uplift (elevation due to natural causes), and erosion.

Welcome to Sitka

ANSWER: C

Sitka, Alaska

WHEN PEOPLE THINK OF AMERICA'S BIGGEST CITIES, PLACES LIKE NEW YORK CITY OR CHICAGO PROBABLY COME TO MIND. But when measured by land area rather than population, the winner is the remote city of Sitka, Alaska. **Sitka covers an area of about 2,870 square miles (7,433 sq km), and encompasses a huge chunk of Alaska's coastline.** The city sits on Baranof Island and part of Chichagof Island in the Alexander Archipelago. Even though the city takes up a lot of space, its population is only about 8,800 people. **By population size, America's largest city would actually be New York City,** with its 8.6 million people—a number that's expected to climb to 9 million by 2040.

Instant Genius

The four largest U.S. cities by area are all in the state of Alaska.

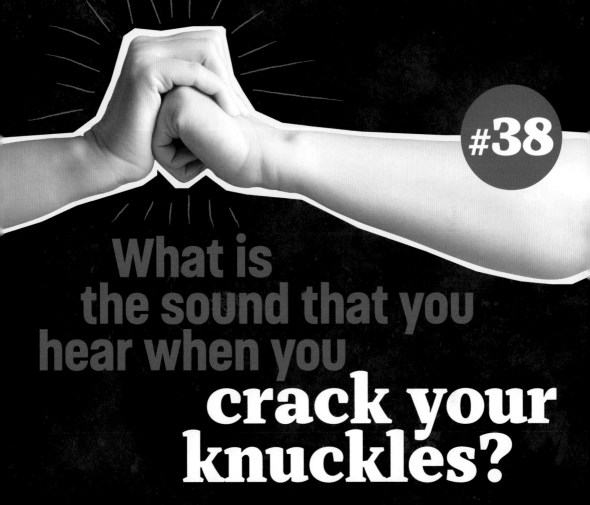

#38

What is the sound that you hear when you crack your knuckles?

a. bones clicking

b. gas bubbles bursting

c. joints realigning themselves

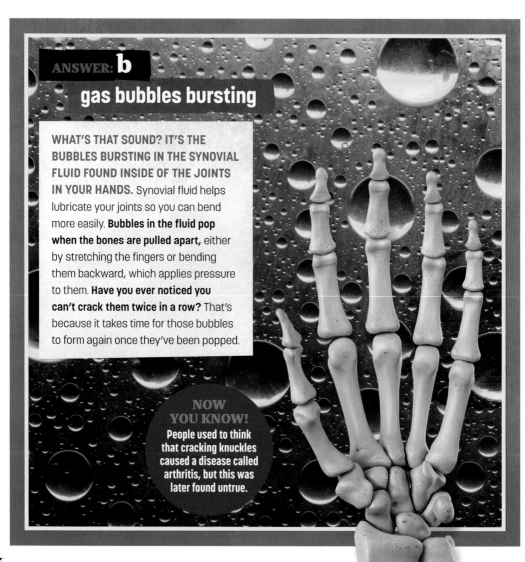

ANSWER: b

gas bubbles bursting

WHAT'S THAT SOUND? IT'S THE BUBBLES BURSTING IN THE SYNOVIAL FLUID FOUND INSIDE OF THE JOINTS IN YOUR HANDS. Synovial fluid helps lubricate your joints so you can bend more easily. **Bubbles in the fluid pop when the bones are pulled apart,** either by stretching the fingers or bending them backward, which applies pressure to them. **Have you ever noticed you can't crack them twice in a row?** That's because it takes time for those bubbles to form again once they've been popped.

NOW YOU KNOW!
People used to think that cracking knuckles caused a disease called arthritis, but this was later found untrue.

Which big cat is the rarest?

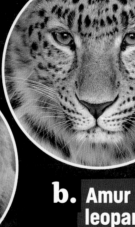

a. African lion

b. Amur leopard

c. Siberian tiger

ANSWER: b

Amur leopard

THE AMUR LEOPARD, NATIVE TO RUSSIA, CHINA, AND NORTH KOREA, was not considered its own species until 2001. What took so long? This species is extremely rare. **Due to poaching and habitat destruction caused by climate change, likely fewer than 100 of these leopards are left in the wild.** When genetic tests found that the Amur leopard was genetically different from other leopards, it became clear that this big cat was its own species in need of protection. **Thank goodness, conservation efforts in recent years have worked, and this big cat's population has jumped by 50 percent.**

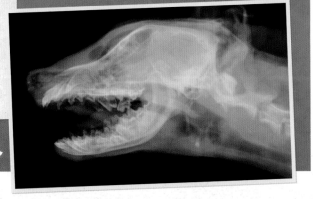

JUST LIKE HUMANS, DOGS ARE BORN WITHOUT VISIBLE TEETH and grow a set of "baby teeth" as they develop. Although humans have a full set of 20 baby teeth by the time they are 3 years old, **dogs usually have about 28 little teeth by the time they are 5 to 6 weeks old.** When these pups reach about 12 weeks old, their teeth start to fall out, and continue to fall out until they are about 6 months old. You might discover one on the ground or in the couch cushions, but it's more **common for puppies to swallow their teeth while they're eating!** Young dogs love to explore the world with their mouths. That's why puppies chew on everything they can get their mouths on. **This process is known as teething and continues until all of their adult teeth grow in.**

Instant Genius

Fully grown dogs have 42 teeth. Humans have 32.

X-ray of a dog's skull showing both baby and adult teeth. →

#41

89

ANSWER: False

A DAY IS MEASURED BY HOW LONG IT TAKES FOR A PLANET TO MAKE ONE COMPLETE ROTATION ON ITS AXIS. Mars rotates about 40 minutes slower than Earth, **so one day on Mars lasts about 40 minutes longer than a day on Earth.** If humans wanted to live on Mars one day, the similar length of day would ease the transition. Both planets also have a similar seasonal pattern. **Like on Earth, daylight hours during summer on Mars are long and daylight hours in winter are short.** However, temperatures on Mars can dip as low as −220 °F (−140 °C), so if humans ever do inhabit the Red Planet, they'll need to find a way to stay warm!

Instant Genius

A season on Mars is twice as long as one on Earth, because Mars is farther from the sun.

NOW YOU KNOW!

Mars is commonly known as Earth's twin because of the similar shape, rotation, and landforms.

Which vertebrate is the most toxic?

a. Gila monster

b. Eastern coral snake

c. Golden poison frog

I'm the king of poison.

ANSWER: **C**

Golden poison frog

THE GOLDEN POISON FROG IS THE MOST LETHAL VERTEBRATE ON THE PLANET. Many frogs have poison-producing skin, but this one takes the gold medal when it comes to toxicity. These amphibians live in the rainforests of western Columbia in South America. **At only 2 inches (5 cm) long, this cute-looking critter could easily sit in the palm of your hand.** But that would be a very big mistake. **A single frog contains enough poison to kill 20,000 mice or 10 people,** so even touching it could make you sick!

NOW YOU KNOW!
Poison frogs are brightly colored to warn predators not to eat them.

Strawberry poison-dart frog

In which year did women start participating in the

Olympic Games?

a. 1896   b. 1900   c. 1926

1900

THE MODERN OLYMPIC GAMES BEGAN IN 1894 AND WERE LIMITED TO MALE ATHLETES. The men who created the Olympics thought that women were too delicate to be participating in athletics, and banned them from competing. **However, in 1900, women were allowed to compete in certain events, such as horseback riding, tennis, and ice-skating.** Charlotte Cooper, a British tennis player in the 1900 Olympic Games, was the first of 22 women competing that year to win a gold medal. Founded in 1921, **the International Women's Sports Federation got involved to fight for women's right to participate in every sport** showcased at the Olympics. Although the gender imbalance within the Olympic Games slowly improved, **it didn't become mandatory to allow women to compete in every sport offered at the Olympics until 2007.**

Jeux Olympiques

EXPOSITION PARIS 1900

PARIS 1900

Charlotte Cooper

Instant Genius

In the Tokyo 2020 Olympics Games, 5,494 women and 5,982 men competed.

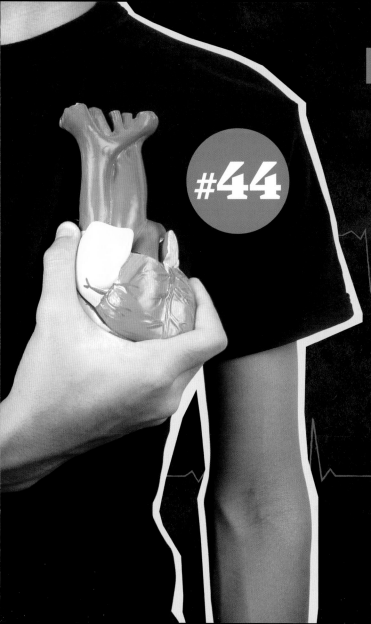

Your
heart
cannot
beat
unless
it's
inside
your
body.

#44

ANSWER: False

THE HEART IS ONE OF THE MOST IMPORTANT ORGANS IN THE ENTIRE BODY because it circulates blood, oxygen, and nutrients through the bloodstream. The heart beats 100,000 times a day, and **it can circulate as much as 1.5 gallons (5.7 L) of blood in just one minute.** If the heart is removed from the body for any amount of time, it stops functioning completely. However, doctors have discovered a way to keep it going on its own. Called "beating heart" technology, **the system keeps the heart alive by holding it in a device that mimics the functions of the body.** This warm "heart in a box" is flooded with blood and oxygen to **keep the heart beating for up to 6 hours on its own.** The technology was developed to keep hearts viable for transplant from donors to recipients.

Instant Genius

The average heart is as big as two hands clasped together.

#45

What kind of business did **Nintendo** start as?

a. an amusement ride manufacturer

b. a trading card company

c. a bubble gum producer

ANSWER: **b**

a trading card company

NINTENDO HAS BEEN AROUND FOR MORE THAN 130 YEARS. In 1889, the founder of the company, Fusajiro Yamauchi, started Nintendo to manufacture hanafuda cards, or flower cards. **Hanafuda cards are traditional Japanese playing cards** made with 12 suits of four cards each, all illustrated with beautiful floral designs. But as time moved forward, so did the company, growing bigger and bigger. **Eventually, in 1978, Nintendo came out with its first arcade game called Computer Othello.** In 1981, when the iconic game *Donkey Kong* was released, Nintendo became a leader in the video game industry. Since then, *Donkey Kong*'s hero, originally named Jumpman, has changed his name to Mario, and **Nintendo has now made more than 700 games.**

What are **baby rabbits** called?

#46

Cute, obviously!

a. kittens **b.** pups **c.** chicks

ANSWER: a

kittens

CATS AREN'T THE ONLY ONES THAT HAVE KITTENS! Baby rabbits are called kittens, too. All the baby rabbits born at the same time are referred to as a litter. **Rabbit litters have five kittens on average, though litter sizes can range from a single to 12.** In the wild, mother rabbits carry their unborn kittens for roughly a month and have their litters between March and September. **Mother rabbits often have between three and four litters of kittens each year!** They usually dig a hole in the ground and hide the hole with grasses and their own fur to protect their kittens. Mother rabbits only feed their kittens at dusk and dawn, so it's rare to see a mother rabbit leave her den. **At three weeks old, when they're about the size of tennis balls, kittens leave the nest.**

Instant Genius
Baby hares are called leverets.

True or False:

Chinese New Year

is always in March.

#47

101

ANSWER: False

CHINESE NEW YEAR, OR LUNAR NEW YEAR, IS AN ANNUAL 15-DAY-LONG FESTIVAL celebrated in Chinese communities all around the world that **always begins with the appearance of the new moon between January 21 and February 20.** The precise calendar date changes from year to year. Festivities continue for 15 days until the next full moon, with lots of feasting, dancing, and singing. **The origins of Chinese New Year come from an ancient legend about a terrible monster named Nián,** which would attack villagers at the beginning of each new year, bringing bad luck upon all of China. To protect themselves, the villagers used loud noises, bright lights, and the color red to scare off the beast until the following year. **Today, people celebrate by dressing in red and setting off fireworks to bring luck in the new year.**

HAPPY NEW YEAR!
USA
33

What was **George Washington Carver's** claim to fame?

#48

a. He revolutionized southern farming.

b. He won a duel against Alexander Hamilton.

c. He invented the helicopter.

ANSWER: a

He revolutionized southern farming.

Peanut seedling →

AS A KID BORN IN THE 1860s, GEORGE WASHINGTON CARVER SPENT HIS TIME LEARNING ABOUT PLANTS AND ANIMALS, and taking on whatever work he could find. He worked his way through high school and earned two college degrees. **Then Carver got a job leading the agricultural department at Tuskegee Normal and Industrial Institute,** where he studied ways that farmers in the Deep South could improve their crops. He learned that cotton crops, which had been grown for years, took nutrients out of the soil. **He had an idea to plant peanuts, sweet potatoes, and soybeans to give nutrients back to the soil—and it worked!** But not many people wanted these new plants. So, Carver figured out how to make new products from the plants, including milk, ink, flour, soap, and molasses. **He made about 300 different products from peanuts alone!**

NOW YOU KNOW!
Established in 1943, George Washington Carver National Monument is the first site in the National Park System named after a Black man.

Houseflies can find sugar with their feet.

Mango, my favorite!

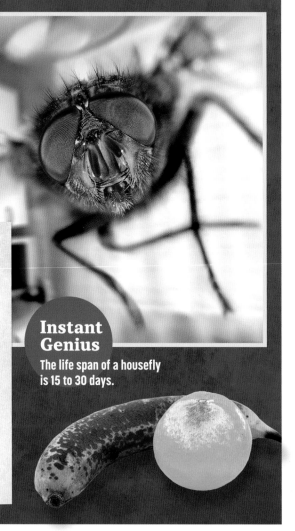

ANSWER: True

FLIES CAN TASTE THEIR FOOD JUST BY WALKING ON IT. That's because they have taste receptors on their feet that **let them sample their meal before really digging in.** Why do they do this? They are looking for important nutrients such as sugars and fats. When they find something they like, they can't just chow down **because flies can't chew.** Instead, they have to dissolve solids into liquids before they can eat. **Flies do this by throwing up digestive juices that break down food and allow them to drink their meal.** Flies usually eat decaying organic stuff and sometimes drink blood from animals.

Instant Genius

The life span of a housefly is 15 to 30 days.

106

50

What did the
Richter scale
measure?

a. depth of the ocean

b. intensity of an earthquake

c. force of a volcanic lava flow

intensity of an earthquake

THE SEVERITY OF EARTHQUAKES WAS ONCE RECORDED USING THE RICHTER SCALE. Charles Richter, who studied earthquakes and volcanoes, developed the tool in 1935. **It was a simple yet precise way to describe the intensity of an earthquake, with a scale ranging from 1 to 10.** The higher the number, the bigger the ground vibration. The scale measured the magnitude, or size, of an earthquake's largest energy jolt. However, it worked better in some areas than others. Today, we use the moment magnitude scale, which also ranges from 1 to 10. **Unlike the Richter scale, the moment magnitude scale measures the total energy released by an earthquake.** So far, no earthquake has ever ranked 10 on any scale, but **the world's most massive quake occurred in Chile in 1960 and reached a terrifying magnitude 9.5.**

Macroseismic Intensity Map
USGS ShakeMap: 1960 Great Chilean Earthquake (Valdivia Earthquake)
May 22, 1960 19:11:20 UTC M9.5 S38.14 W73.41 Depth: 25.0km
ID:official19600522191120_30

Intensity map of the 1960 Valdivia earthquake in Chile

Not felt	Weak	Light	Moderate	Strong	Very strong	Severe	Violent	Extreme
None	None	None	Very light	Light	Moderate	Moderate/heavy	Heavy	Very heavy
<0.05	0.3	2.76	6.2	11.5	21.5	40.1	74.7	>139
<0.02	0.13	1.41	4.65	9.64	20	41.4	85.8	>178
I	II-III	IV	V	VI	VII	VIII	IX	X+

n Worden et al. (2012)
trument ○ Reported Intensity   ★ Epicenter ▭ Rupture
Version 1: Processed 2019-09-26T00:50:04Z

Instant Genius

Nearly 50 earthquakes occur each day, and most go unnoticed.

Valdivia, Chile, after the 1960 earthquake

NOW YOU KNOW!

Earthquakes occur when tectonic plates—chunks of land that make up Earth's crust—move. More severe earthquakes occur when one tectonic plate is forced beneath another.

What **historical document**

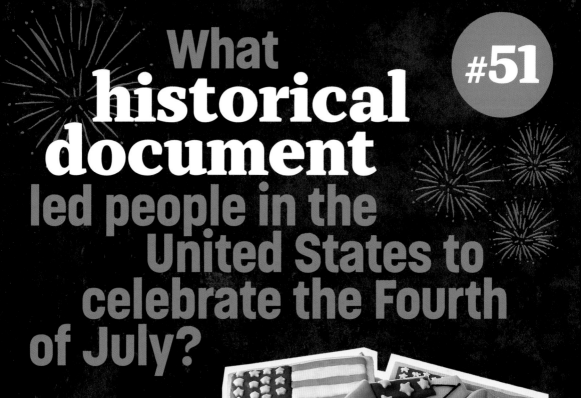

led people in the United States to celebrate the Fourth of July?

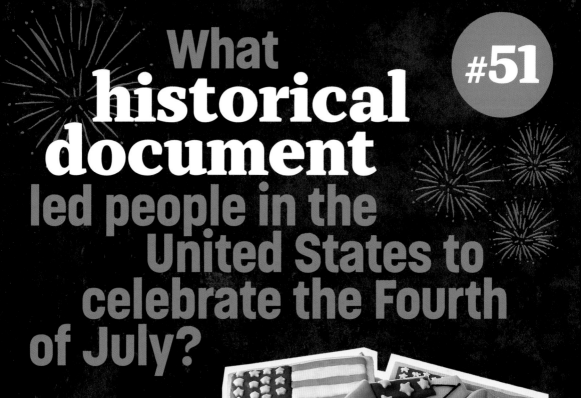

a. the Constitution

b. the Declaration of Independence

c. the Bill of Rights

ANSWER: b

the Declaration of Independence

THE DECLARATION OF INDEPENDENCE, SIGNED IN 1776, was the first step toward establishing what is now the United States of America. **On June 11, the Continental Congress tasked a group of men, led by Thomas Jefferson, to write this declaration,** informing the British government that the American colonies wanted freedom from the British Empire. For the next few weeks, a group of five men—Thomas Jefferson, Benjamin Franklin, Robert R. Livingston, John Adams, and Roger Sherman—worked on a draft. **Then on July 4, 1776, the 56 congressional delegates came together to approve the Declaration of Independence.**

NOW YOU KNOW!
Thomas Jefferson went on to be an important figure in American history, allying the colonists with the French to defeat the British Empire. He later became America's third president in 1801.

True or False:

Earth's moon once had **water.**

#52

111

SOFIA (Stratospheric Observatory for Infrared Astronomy) mounted on a Boeing 747.

NASA

DLR

N747NA

ANSWER: **True**

IN 2020, NASA LAUNCHED THE EXPLORATORY ROBOT SOFIA TO EVALUATE THE MOON'S SURFACE AND CRATERS. While looking deep into one of the moon's biggest craters, SOFIA found traces of water. **Then, at the bottom of Clavius crater—one of the biggest craters we can see from Earth—they found evidence of more water!** Scientists aren't totally sure where it came from, but they think there could be a few explanations: For example, perhaps meteorites that regularly crashed into the moon dispersed the water across the moon's surface because of its lack of atmosphere. **However, there's only evidence of extremely small amounts of water.** The Sahara desert has 100 times the amount of water that scientists have found on the moon.

Clavius crater

NOW YOU KNOW!
For a long time, scientists couldn't tell moon water from its close cousin, hydroxyl, because the samples were so small.

#53

How quickly can your brain identify an image?

a. 13 milliseconds

b. 0.3 seconds

c. 3 seconds

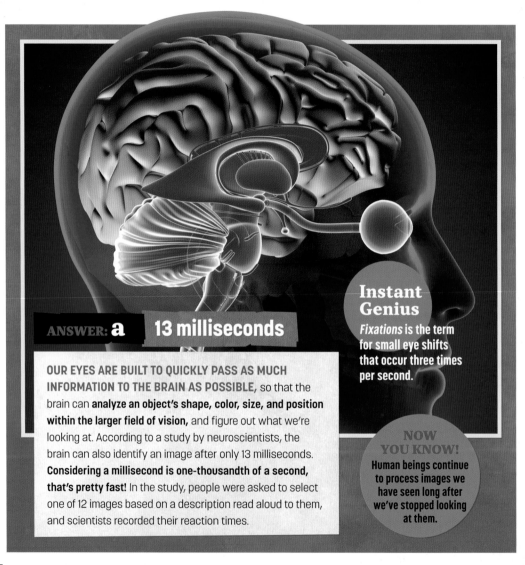

ANSWER: a **13 milliseconds**

OUR EYES ARE BUILT TO QUICKLY PASS AS MUCH INFORMATION TO THE BRAIN AS POSSIBLE, so that the brain can **analyze an object's shape, color, size, and position within the larger field of vision,** and figure out what we're looking at. According to a study by neuroscientists, the brain can also identify an image after only 13 milliseconds. **Considering a millisecond is one-thousandth of a second, that's pretty fast!** In the study, people were asked to select one of 12 images based on a description read aloud to them, and scientists recorded their reaction times.

Which animal is an ungulate?

a. horse

b. caterpillar

c. octopus

AN UNGULATE IS A MAMMAL WITH HOOVES, which are on the tips of their toes and help the animals move by sturdily supporting their body weight. **There are both odd-toed and even-toed ungulates.** Odd-toed ungulates include horses (which have one toe), rhinos (which have three toes), and tapirs (which have four toes on the front feet, and three toes on the hind feet). Even-toed ungulates include two-toed camels and giraffes, and four-toed hippos. What else do these animals have in common? **Most ungulates are herbivores.** In recent years, **ungulate populations have risen because animals that eat them, such as wolves, tigers, and leopards, have dropped in numbers.**

NOW YOU KNOW!
The squishy triangle-shaped part of a horse's foot is called a frog.

Tapir

Hippo

116

#55

True or False:

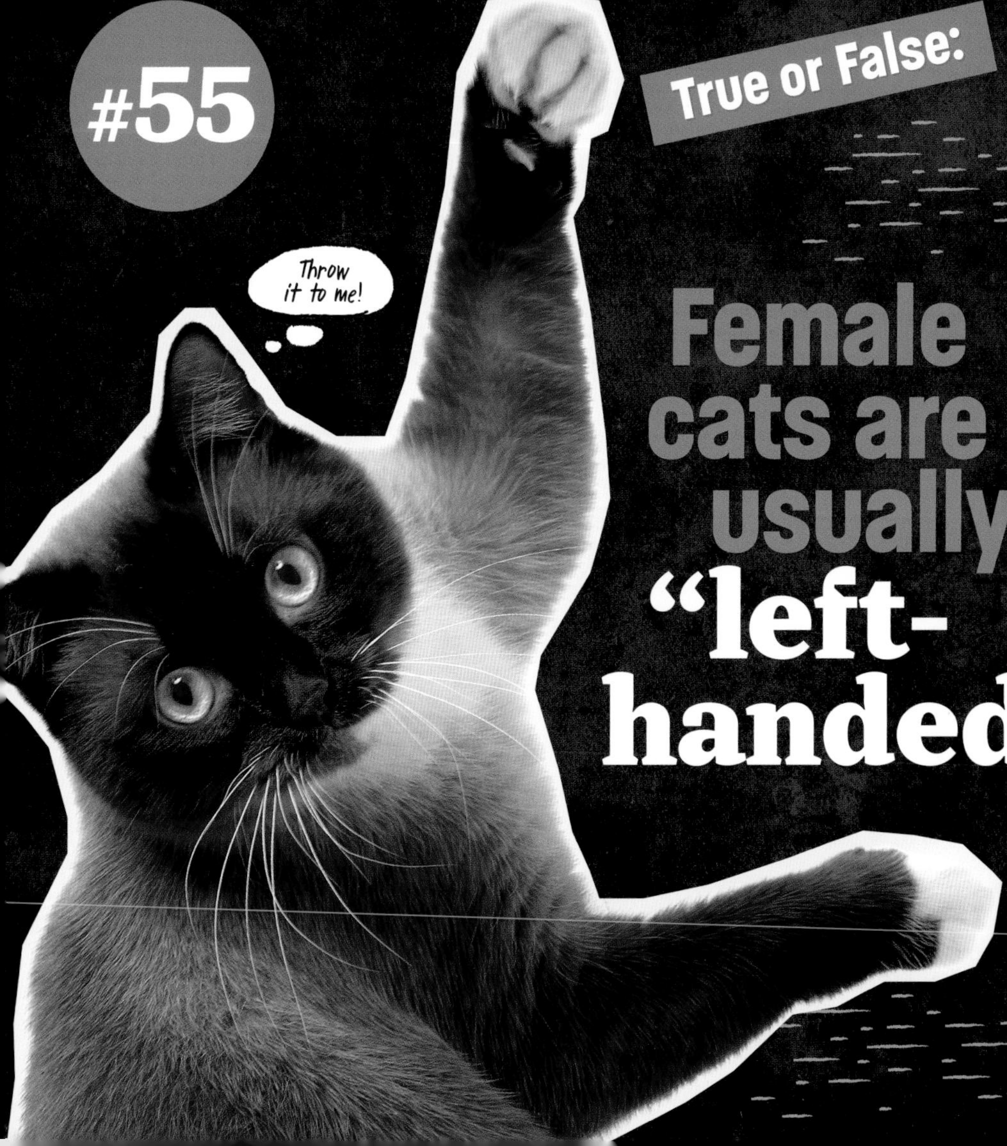

Female cats are usually "left-handed."

IN THE SAME WAY THAT HUMANS HAVE A PREFERENCE FOR USING THEIR RIGHT OR LEFT HAND, animals appear to be the same. Scientists have conducted a series of studies over the past 50 years to examine how cats do certain things such as walking around, knocking things over, and reaching for food. From their research, **they determined that male cats do most things with their left paws in the lead, and female cats do most things with their right paws.** Their conclusion: Paw preference might be linked to gender markers in the cat's genes. **These preference behaviors can also be seen with other animals like dogs and horses, and humans, too.**

NOW YOU KNOW!
Scientists also noticed that lefty animals—and ambidextrous animals, who used both paws equally—exhibited more stress, but the reason why is still a mystery.

Instant Genius
With humans, males are about 2 percent more likely to be left-hand dominant than females.

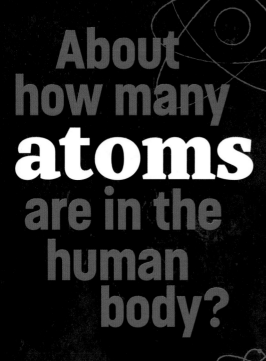

About how many **atoms** are in the human body?

a. **700,000**

b. **700,000,000**

c. **7,000,000,000,000,000,000,000,000,000**

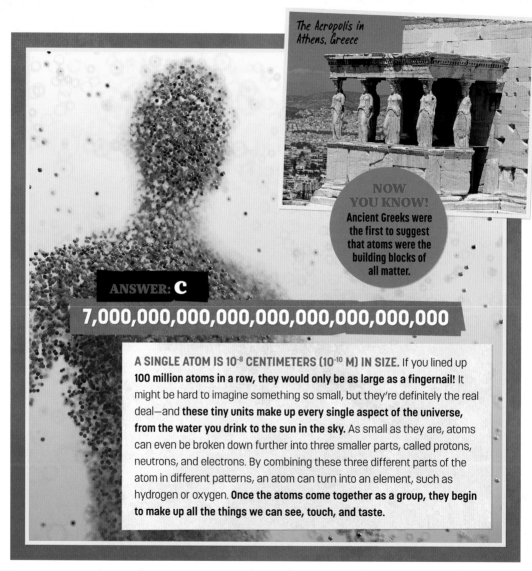

The Acropolis in Athens, Greece

ANSWER: C

7,000,000,000,000,000,000,000,000,000

A SINGLE ATOM IS 10^{-8} CENTIMETERS (10^{-10} M) IN SIZE. If you lined up **100 million atoms in a row, they would only be as large as a fingernail!** It might be hard to imagine something so small, but they're definitely the real deal—and **these tiny units make up every single aspect of the universe, from the water you drink to the sun in the sky.** As small as they are, atoms can even be broken down further into three smaller parts, called protons, neutrons, and electrons. By combining these three different parts of the atom in different patterns, an atom can turn into an element, such as hydrogen or oxygen. **Once the atoms come together as a group, they begin to make up all the things we can see, touch, and taste.**

#57

True or False:

The world's **first** **photo** was taken by the **sun.**

ANSWER: **True**

THE WORLD'S FIRST PHOTOGRAPH WAS TAKEN IN 1826 OR 1827 BY A FRENCH INVENTOR NAMED JOSEPH NICÉPHORE NIÉPCE. This first photograph, which **shows the courtyard of Niépce's country home,** is very different from today's modern pictures made with a digital camera. Instead, it is a heliograph, or "sun drawing." To create the heliograph, **Niépce used a box-shaped device with a tiny hole to expose a pewter plate to light and radiation from the sun.** The plate had been treated with a chemical solution made up of lavender oil and asphalt. **The end result, which took 8 hours to produce, was quite dark and blurry.** You would have to look closely to see the image, but it's considered so valuable that it hangs in a museum.

Instant Genius
The first digital camera was created in 1975.

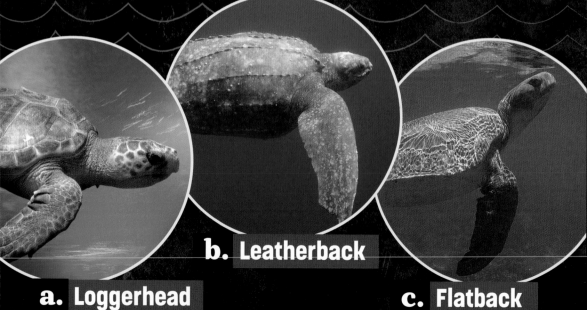

Which sea turtle #58
has a
soft shell?

b. Leatherback

a. Loggerhead

c. Flatback

Instant Genius

Sea turtles can live up to 50 years.

ANSWER: b

Leatherback

UNLIKE OTHER SEA TURTLES, LEATHERBACKS DO NOT HAVE A HARD SHELL. Instead, their carapace is made up of **thousands of bony plates covered with a dark, leathery skin.** The flexible shell has ridges that help leatherbacks smoothly glide through water and **dive deeper than any other sea turtle species, down to 4,200 feet (1,280 m).** Because they're cold-blooded, they can stay down in such deep water for 85 minutes. Leatherbacks are the largest sea turtle species, **weighing up to 2,000 pounds (907 kg) and stretching 7 feet (2 m) long.** Leatherbacks live in the Atlantic, Indian, and Pacific Oceans, and the Mediterranean Sea. Leatherbacks are also unique in that they migrate farther than any other reptile in the world.

NOW YOU KNOW!

The leatherback sea turtle is the largest of the seven sea turtle species and the largest turtle in the world. The other sea turtle species are called loggerhead, Kemp's ridley, green, olive ridley, hawksbill, and flatback.

True or False:

Earth is the only planet in our solar system not named after an **ancient god.**

#59

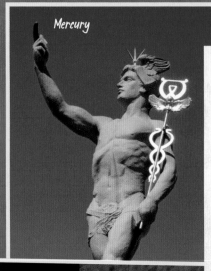
Mercury

MERCURY, VENUS, MARS, JUPITER, AND SATURN ARE ALL VISIBLE WITH THE NAKED EYE. The names we use for these planets come from the ancient Romans, who named them after legendary gods and goddesses. **Mercury was the god of travel, Venus was the goddess of love, Mars was the god of war, Jupiter was the king of the gods, and Saturn was the god of agriculture.** The farthest planets in our solar system were discovered later, but the naming convention continued. **Uranus was a Greek name for the father of the Titans, and Neptune was named after the god of the sea.** The only planet that doesn't follow this tradition is Earth. **Instead, our planet's name has Germanic roots and means "the ground."**

Neptune

Venetia Burney

NOW YOU KNOW!
An ancient Greek mathematician and philosopher named Ptolemy was one of the first people to use math to explain how the planets move.

Instant Genius
The dwarf planet Pluto was named by an 11-year-old girl after the god of the underworld.

126

Why are basketballs orange?

a. to use the inventor's favorite color

b. to make them easy to see

c. to look different from soccer balls

to make them easy to see

WHEN BASKETBALL WAS INVENTED IN SPRINGFIELD, MASSACHUSETTS, IN 1891, the original balls used to play the game were soccer balls. Thirty years after the game was invented, the first international games were played. **Eventually, companies began designing and selling balls specifically for basketball.** These first basketballs were brown and difficult to spot on the court for both the players and the observers. In the 1950s, Butler University basketball coach **Tony Hinkle solved this problem by introducing the orange-colored basketball to—you guessed it—keep your eye on the ball.**

Original ball

Goose Tatum of the Harlem Globetrotters holds a basketball in one hand in a locker room, 1951.

Instant Genius

The first baskets used for basketball were peach baskets.

128

What do bottlenose dolphins do to track prey?

a. click **b.** do backflips **c.** play dead

I smell dinner!

#61

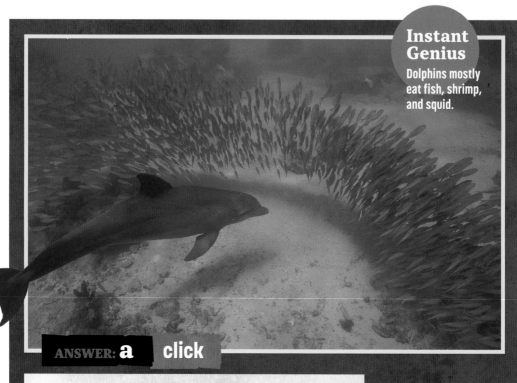

Instant Genius

Dolphins mostly eat fish, shrimp, and squid.

ANSWER: a **click**

BOTTLENOSE DOLPHINS MAKE A CLICKING SOUND WHEN THEY ARE TRACKING THEIR PREY. They click through fat-filled lumps of tissue called the dorsal bursae. The sound wave of the click bounces off their prey and back to the dolphin. **From the echo, dolphins can learn the size, location, and shape of the prey.** This dolphin detective work is called echolocation. Echolocation can also be used to track predators. Dolphins are also social and can be very playful. **They live together in groups and communicate with one another in whistles, squeaks, and clicks.** Bottlenose dolphins can be very noisy when they want to be!

NOW YOU KNOW!
There are 36 species of dolphins, ranging in size from 5 to 32 feet (1.5–10 m) and weighing up to 6 tons (5,443 kg)!

#62

In Mexico, who is celebrated during **Day of the Dead?**

a. Aztec gods

b. dead loved ones

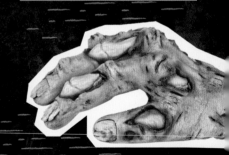

c. zombies

ANSWER: b **dead loved ones**

DÍA DE LOS MUERTOS, OR DAY OF THE DEAD, IS A MAJOR HOLIDAY IN MEXICAN CULTURE, honoring loved ones and celebrating the lives of those who have passed away. The holiday takes place over two days on November 1 and 2. **To start, families come together to clean the graves of their loved ones** before making an altar called an *ofrenda*. On the altars, they place pictures of the deceased, along with their loved ones' favorite foods and drinks. **Then they enjoy a full night of singing and dancing.** The holiday comes from the traditions of the Aztec, Toltec, and other Indigenous people from Mexico. **They believe that, because a person can live on in the afterlife, there's no need to be so sad.**

#63

How many light-years would it take to cross the **Milky Way galaxy?**

a. 1,000 light-years

b. 100,000 light-years

c. 1,000,000 light-years

ANSWER: b

100,000 light-years

LIGHT IS THE FASTEST THING IN THE UNIVERSE. Scientists measure **how fast light can travel by measuring the distance light can go in a single year.** (This is where the term *light-year* comes from.) The reason scientists use light-years as a unit of measurement in space is because **light travels through space at a speed of 186,000 miles (300,000 km) per second.** That's like 66 trips across the United States in one second! **Earth is about 8 light-minutes from the sun,** and to travel to the very edge of our solar system, into the farthest reaches of the Oort cloud, it would take about 1.87 light-years.

Instant Genius

To get to the nearest star, Proxima Centauri, it would take 4.25 light-years.

True or False: **Bones weigh more** than muscles.

#64

ANSWER: False

BONES ARE ALWAYS LIGHTER THAN MUSCLES BECAUSE OF THEIR COMPOSITION. Bones are made of hard calcium on the outside. But they are filled with bone marrow on the inside, which has a coral-like consistency, making bones less dense and heavy. **Muscles are heavier and denser than bones because they are made of fibers and tissues filled with blood,** which helps the body move. Tendons connect our muscles to our bones. **During childhood, new parts of the bone are added to the skeleton.** Usually this happens at such a fast rate that new bone is made faster than the old bone can be removed. But once a person reaches the age of about 30, new bone production slows and then stops altogether. **Muscles peak in growth around the age of 40, and start to weaken as usage declines.**

Instant Genius

Bones and teeth are where more than 99 percent of the body's calcium is stored.

How do **insects** breathe?

a. through their mouths

b. through their noses

c. through their abdomens

through their abdomens

INSECTS BREATHE THROUGH LITTLE HOLES IN THEIR THORAX AND ABDOMEN CALLED SPIRACLES, which can open and close. The air they take in spreads through little tubes in the insects' bodies. Unlike humans and other mammals, **bugs don't have lungs. Instead, they transport air directly to their muscles and tissues through these tubes.** Insects inhale oxygen and exhale carbon dioxide, just like humans—sending carbon dioxide through the same tiny tubes and out the spiracles that take in oxygen. **Compared to their body size, insects inhale a lot more oxygen than mammals do.** Although people can only hold their breath for a few minutes, some insects can last for several hours!

Scanning electron micrograph of a fruit fly spiracle

Instant Genius
Insects cannot pant.

NOW YOU KNOW!
Scientists can learn about insect respiration through new X-ray machines that allow them to examine bugs breathing in real time.

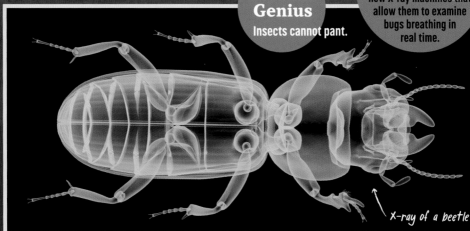

X-ray of a beetle

66

Is 0 an **odd** or **even** number?

a. It's odd. **b.** It's even. **c.** It's both.

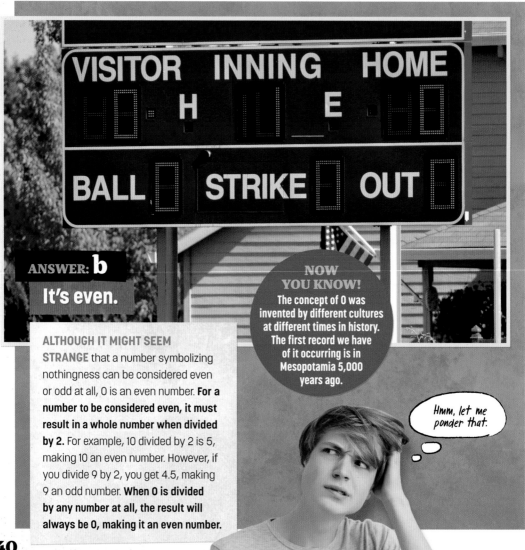

VISITOR   INNING   HOME

H   E

BALL   STRIKE   OUT

ANSWER: b

It's even.

ALTHOUGH IT MIGHT SEEM STRANGE that a number symbolizing nothingness can be considered even or odd at all, 0 is an even number. **For a number to be considered even, it must result in a whole number when divided by 2.** For example, 10 divided by 2 is 5, making 10 an even number. However, if you divide 9 by 2, you get 4.5, making 9 an odd number. **When 0 is divided by any number at all, the result will always be 0, making it an even number.**

NOW YOU KNOW!
The concept of 0 was invented by different cultures at different times in history. The first record we have of it occurring is in Mesopotamia 5,000 years ago.

Hmm, let me ponder that.

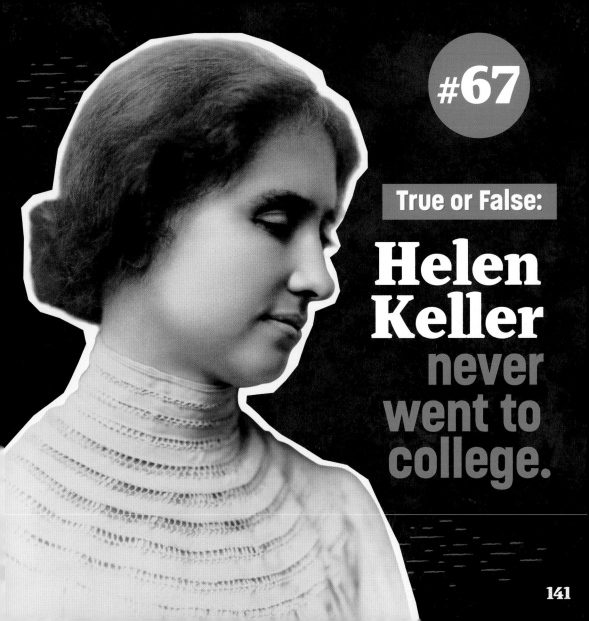

#67

True or False:

Helen Keller

never went to college.

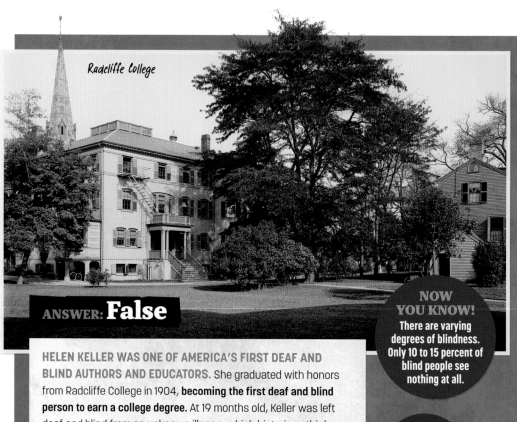

Radcliffe College

ANSWER: **False**

HELEN KELLER WAS ONE OF AMERICA'S FIRST DEAF AND BLIND AUTHORS AND EDUCATORS. She graduated with honors from Radcliffe College in 1904, **becoming the first deaf and blind person to earn a college degree.** At 19 months old, Keller was left deaf and blind from an unknown illness, which historians think could have been scarlet fever. When Keller was six, she was sent to the Perkins Institution for the Blind, where **she learned to communicate using Braille and sign language.** Once she received the proper accommodations, she quickly excelled in her education. **For much of her adult life, Keller was a teacher and a disability rights activist,** calling for better treatment of deaf and blind people. In 1920, she cofounded the American Civil Liberties Union, which is still active today in defending and preserving individuals' rights.

Instant Genius

Helen Keller was good friends with famous people like Mark Twain, Eleanor Roosevelt, and Alexander Graham Bell.

Roughly how many people **apply to be astronauts** during each recruiting cycle?

#68

a. 10–20

b. 10,000–20,000

c. 1–2 million

ANSWER: **b**

10,000–20,000

NASA's 2017 Astronaut Candidate Class

NASA SELECTS ASTRONAUTS ROUGHLY EVERY TWO YEARS.
Since the moon landing in 1969, interest in space has grown steadily, leading more young kids to dream of becoming astronauts when they grow up. **In 2017, more than 18,000 people applied to join NASA's astronaut program, setting a new record.** In 2020, roughly 12,000 people applied. NASA has rigorous requirements to become an astronaut. **Applicants must be U.S. citizens** and must pass an intensive physical exam just to be considered. **They need not only a bachelor's degree, but also a master's degree in engineering, science, or other related subject,** as well as two years of related experience. Potential **astronauts must also be strong leaders who can work well in a team and communicate clearly,** because it requires an incredible amount of coordination to launch, maintain, and land a spaceship.

Instant Genius

Once accepted, an astronaut can take two years to be fully trained.

Which animal is the most successful hunter?

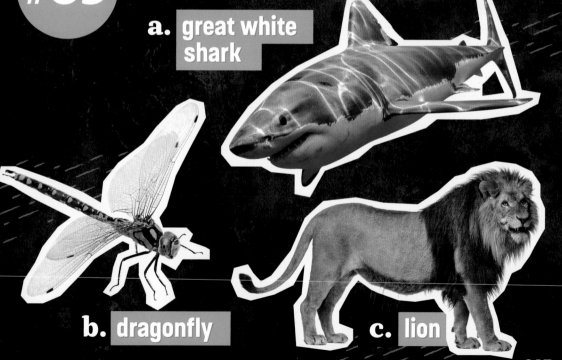

a. **great white shark**

b. **dragonfly**

c. **lion**

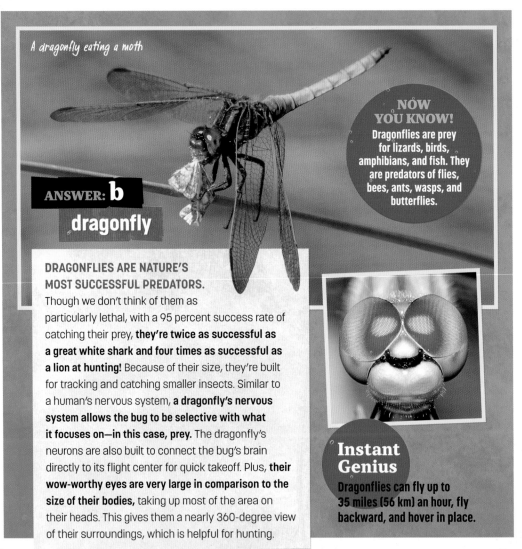

A dragonfly eating a moth

ANSWER: b

dragonfly

DRAGONFLIES ARE NATURE'S MOST SUCCESSFUL PREDATORS.
Though we don't think of them as particularly lethal, with a 95 percent success rate of catching their prey, **they're twice as successful as a great white shark and four times as successful as a lion at hunting!** Because of their size, they're built for tracking and catching smaller insects. Similar to a human's nervous system, **a dragonfly's nervous system allows the bug to be selective with what it focuses on—in this case, prey.** The dragonfly's neurons are also built to connect the bug's brain directly to its flight center for quick takeoff. Plus, **their wow-worthy eyes are very large in comparison to the size of their bodies,** taking up most of the area on their heads. This gives them a nearly 360-degree view of their surroundings, which is helpful for hunting.

Instant Genius

Dragonflies can fly up to 35 miles (56 km) an hour, fly backward, and hover in place.

70

True or False:

Break dancing
is an Olympic sport.

147

Instant Genius

Breaking, b-boying, and *b-girling* are other terms for break dancing.

Break dancers in St. Petersburg, Russia

ANSWER: True

BREAK DANCING ISN'T JUST A FAMOUS HIP-HOP DANCE STYLE. Starting with the 2024 Paris Games, it's been elevated to the status of an Olympic sport! **For years, the International Olympic Committee has looked for ways to increase its popularity** with younger and more diverse audiences. That's why they've also added sports such as skateboarding, surfing, and sport climbing in recent years. **Breaking is a grassroots acrobatic dance style that was first performed in city streets in the 1970s.** Breakers do flips and spins, and freeze in poses that seem to defy gravity, all while expressing their individual creativity. Now that's breaking new ground!

How much of the universe is visible from Earth?

a. about 5 percent

b. about 50 percent

c. about 85 percent

about 5 percent

TECHNOLOGY HAS BECOME EXTREMELY ADVANCED OVER THE PAST HUNDRED YEARS, but even with **NASA's most powerful telescopes and satellites, scientists can observe only about 5 percent of the known universe.** As the universe expands, the most distant objects in space move even farther away, and the light from them takes longer to reach us. **Until the light from an object reaches us, we don't know that something is there.** Scientists estimate that the observable universe includes 2 trillion galaxies. **The rest of this space is filled with an invisible substance known as dark matter and dark energy,** which are somehow connected to the vacuum in space and repel gravity.

NOW YOU KNOW!
Dark matter makes up 25 percent of the observable universe, and dark energy makes up 70 percent.

The James Webb Space Telescope

Constructing the James Webb Space Telescope at NASA's Goddard Space Flight Center in Greenbelt, MD, 2017

How fast do **nerve impulses** travel to and from the brain?

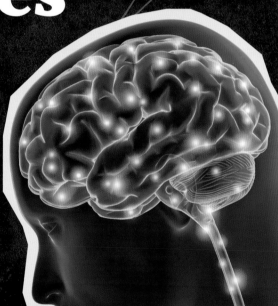

a. 75 miles (121 km) an hour

b. 268 miles (431 km) an hour

c. 426 miles (686 km) an hour

151

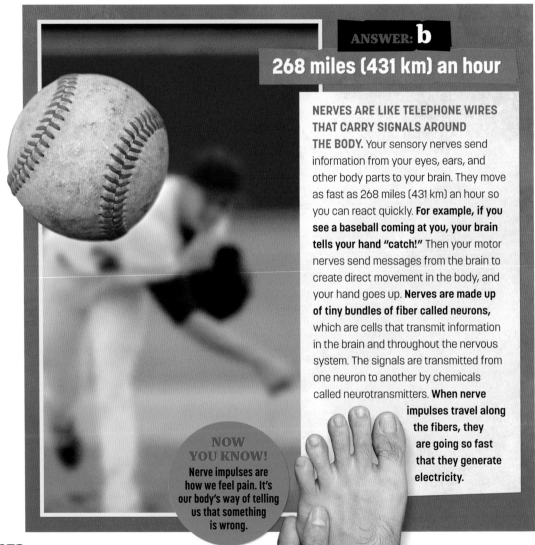

268 miles (431 km) an hour

NERVES ARE LIKE TELEPHONE WIRES THAT CARRY SIGNALS AROUND THE BODY. Your sensory nerves send information from your eyes, ears, and other body parts to your brain. They move as fast as 268 miles (431 km) an hour so you can react quickly. **For example, if you see a baseball coming at you, your brain tells your hand "catch!"** Then your motor nerves send messages from the brain to create direct movement in the body, and your hand goes up. **Nerves are made up of tiny bundles of fiber called neurons,** which are cells that transmit information in the brain and throughout the nervous system. The signals are transmitted from one neuron to another by chemicals called neurotransmitters. **When nerve impulses travel along the fibers, they are going so fast that they generate electricity.**

NOW YOU KNOW!

Nerve impulses are how we feel pain. It's our body's way of telling us that something is wrong.

True or False: There are about **50 million birds on the planet.**

#73

ANSWER: False

THERE ARE 50 *BILLION* BIRDS ON THE PLANET—AT THE VERY LEAST. How do we know? **A biologist took a photo of a flock of swallows and counted 500,000 birds in it.** This made him wonder whether he could estimate the total bird population on Earth. Bird populations are particularly difficult to estimate because they vary a lot in size, and they migrate as well as fly around. So the biologist created a new method for counting that combines data from previous studies with **new data from bird-watchers and amateur citizen scientists— people who aren't scientists but who are interested in science as a hobby.** Together, this covered an estimated 92 percent of the world's avian species. However, 50 billion is the biologist's lowest estimate—his study illustrates that **Earth may have as many as 428 billion birds.**

Instant Genius
There are 25 billion domesticated chickens, which is more than any other bird in the world.

Why do dogs smell each other's rear ends?

a. to inspect each other's tails

b. to claim dominance

c. to greet each other

#74

15

Instant Genius

Dogs rely heavily on body language as well as smell to communicate with one another.

ANSWER: C

to greet each other

ALTHOUGH THIS INSTINCT MAY SEEM GROSS TO HUMANS, IT MAKES PERFECT SENSE TO CANINES. Dogs experience their world primarily through smell, rather than their other senses. **A good sniff from another dog's behind can provide clues about its new friend's health, gender, mood, and diet.** Part of why a dog's sense of smell is so enhanced is thanks to **Jacobson's organ, which is a remarkable smell receptor that spreads from the nasal cavity to the roof of the mouth.** The nerve in the organ leads directly to the dog's brain, and responds to substances their noses can't detect.

NOW YOU KNOW!

Scientists say that a dog's sense of smell is at least 10,000 times better than a human's sense of smell.

If a person weighed 110 pounds (50 kg) on **Earth,** how much would they weigh on **Mars?**

#75

a. 42 pounds (19 kg)

b. 110 pounds (50 kg)

c. 142 pounds (64 kg)

Instant Genius

Mars has two moons that have been pulled into orbit, whereas Earth only has one.

ANSWER: a

42 pounds (19 kg)

This illustration places Mars next to Earth to show size difference between the two planets. Mars is not actually this close to Earth.

OUR WEIGHT CHANGES ON OTHER PLANETS DUE TO GRAVITY. Gravity is the force that pulls objects together—**the more gravity, the more an object will weigh. Gravity is based on the mass of the planet.** Objects with more mass have more gravity, and objects with less mass have less gravity. Thus on Mars, which is smaller than Earth, a 110-pound (50-kg) person would only weigh 42 pounds (19 kg). But on Jupiter, which is much larger than Earth, that same person would weigh a whopping 253 pounds (115 kg). The force of gravity keeps all the planets in orbit around the sun without pulling them in, **and also keeps the moon orbiting around Earth.**

NOW YOU KNOW!
Gravity weakens with distance, so the closer objects are to each other, the stronger their gravitational pull.

What can cause a
tsunami?

a. an earthquake

b. a volcanic eruption

c. both

ENTERING

TSUNAMI HAZARD ZONE

ANSWER: c **both**

A TSUNAMI IS A SERIES OF GIGANTIC WAVES CAUSED BY AN UNDERWATER VOLCANIC ERUPTION OR EARTHQUAKE, or possibly even a meteor crashing into the sea. **These gigantic waves can tower as high as 100 feet (30 m) tall.** About 80 percent of the massive waves occur in an area of the Pacific Ocean called the "Ring of Fire." Though Hawaii is not in the Ring of Fire, it's located in an area that experiences about one tsunami every year, with a severe one occurring every seven years. Thank goodness, scientists have figured out an accurate way to predict when they will happen anywhere on the globe. How? **They calculate the depth of the water, distances between places, and the time of an earthquake** or weather event so they can warn people to seek shelter.

One of the deepwater buoys used in the DART (Deep-ocean Assessment and Reporting of Tsunamis) tsunami warning system

True or False: Some spiders have 12 eyes.

#77

161

MOST SPIDERS HAVE FOUR PAIRS OF EYES, but some can have as many as six pairs—and others have none! **Each pair has a different role.** The front pair has the best quality vision, helping the spider see detail, shapes, and color. The purpose of the peripheral pairs on the sides is to spot motion. **Spiders do not have necks like we do, so having eyes placed all the way around their heads allows them to quickly identify potential predators.** Additionally, spiders often eat small and fast-moving insects, which the eyes on the sides of the body help find. Despite the number of eyes they have, most spider species actually do not rely on them to get around because **their vision is so poor. Instead, they use touch, vibration, and taste to survive.**

78

What is a **zarf?**

a. a scarf for a dog

b. a group of zebras

c. a cardboard sleeve

ANSWER: C

a cardboard sleeve

HAVE YOU EVER ORDERED A HOT CHOCOLATE AND NOTICED A TUBE OR "SLEEVE" made of cardboard around the cup? That's called a zarf! **Zarfs are made for cups holding hot liquids, such as coffee and hot chocolate, to protect people's fingers from burning.** Early versions of zarfs were made as far back as the 1800s in the Middle East, where they were **made of metal and were much fancier and more decorative than they are today.** Cardboard zarfs as we know them today were originally called "Java Jackets."

#79

Which animal has the most **muscles** in its **face?**

a. shark

b. human

c. horse

165

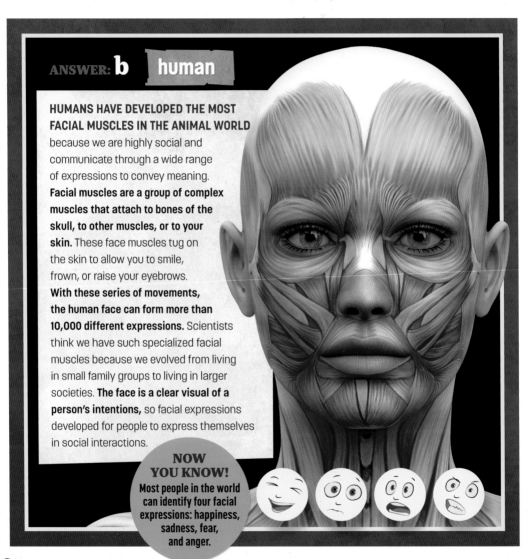

HUMANS HAVE DEVELOPED THE MOST FACIAL MUSCLES IN THE ANIMAL WORLD because we are highly social and communicate through a wide range of expressions to convey meaning. **Facial muscles are a group of complex muscles that attach to bones of the skull, to other muscles, or to your skin.** These face muscles tug on the skin to allow you to smile, frown, or raise your eyebrows. **With these series of movements, the human face can form more than 10,000 different expressions.** Scientists think we have such specialized facial muscles because we evolved from living in small family groups to living in larger societies. **The face is a clear visual of a person's intentions,** so facial expressions developed for people to express themselves in social interactions.

NOW YOU KNOW!
Most people in the world can identify four facial expressions: happiness, sadness, fear, and anger.

Who was the first self-made female millionaire?

a. Dolly Parton

b. Oprah Winfrey

c. Madam C. J. Walker

#80

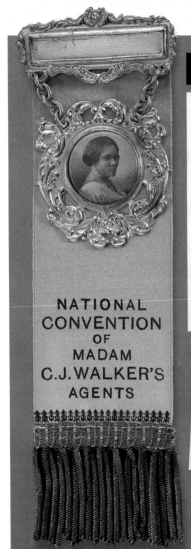

NATIONAL
CONVENTION
OF
MADAM
C.J.WALKER'S
AGENTS

Madam C. J. Walker

BORN ON A LOUISIANA PLANTATION TO ENSLAVED PARENTS IN 1867, Madam C. J. Walker was an orphan at the age of 7. **By 20, she was a widow raising a 3-year-old daughter by herself.** She had little formal education and struggled to support her child. **The stress was so severe that she began to lose her hair. She developed a hair care system to grow back her lost hair, and a new business was born.** Her product was especially helpful for people who were losing their hair from scalp infections. At the time, many Americans didn't have indoor plumbing, making proper hygiene a challenge. **By 1908, Walker was traveling from state to state, training thousands of Black women to be sales agents,** and her business boomed. By the time Walker died in 1919, she was a self-made millionaire.

Madam C. J. Walker and friends in her car, 1911

NOW YOU KNOW!
Alopecia, also known as baldness, is the lack of hair.

True or False:

Cats can see
more colors
than humans do.

#81

CATS SEE THE WORLD DIFFERENTLY THAN WE DO. Compared to what we see, the world is dimmer and blurrier. **Their eyes contain fewer cone cells, which are the parts of the eye that detect color.** A cat can see shades of blue and green, but reds and pinks might also look green, and purples might look blue. However, because their eyes have more light-detecting rod cells, **cats can see much better in dim light and darkness than we can.** Rod cells also refresh more quickly, which gives felines the added **bonus of being able to track rapid movements.** No wonder there are so many hilarious videos of laser-chasing kitties online!

Instant Genius

A cat's field of vision spans 200 degrees, compared to our 180 degrees.

NOW YOU KNOW!
Cats can be speedy in short bursts, reaching speeds of up to 30 miles (48 km) an hour and jumping as high as 5 feet (1.5 m) in the air to capture prey.

How are galaxies categorized?

a. shape **b.** size **c.** location

shape

GALAXIES ARE MASSES OF STARS, GAS, AND DUST HELD TOGETHER BY GRAVITY AND DARK MATTER, a mysterious substance that affects how stars move within galaxies. They are classified by their shape and fall into **three major categories: elliptical, spiral, and irregular.** Each shape category contains vastly different sizes of galaxies, from ones with "only" 100 million stars to those with more than a trillion. **A third of all galaxies are elliptical,** and can include circles and flatter ovals. **Spiral galaxies—like the Milky Way and neighboring Andromeda— look like flat, bluish disks** with yellow bulges in the middle. **Irregular galaxies don't fall into either shape category.** Astronomers believe these were much older and were plentiful in the universe before the elliptical and spiral galaxies started to develop.

Elliptical

Spiral

Irregular

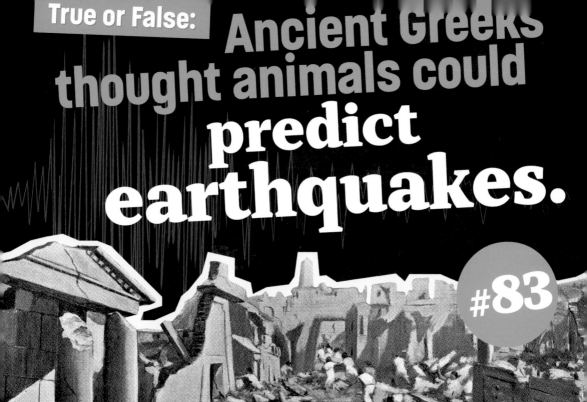

Ancient Greeks thought animals could **predict earthquakes.**

#83

173

There are roughly 500,000 measurable earthquakes each year, but humans detect only a fifth of them.

Thucydides

ANSWER: True

CAN ANIMALS REALLY PREDICT EARTHQUAKES? The short answer: We don't know, but the story that they can has been with us for centuries. In 373 BCE, the ancient Greek historian **Thucydides wrote about how rats, weasels, snakes, and centipedes all fled the city of Helike days before a large earthquake hit the area,** causing massive damage. And today, although animals might not be able to forecast the next quake, they do seem to be sensitive to them when they arrive. **Many pet owners have reported their animals acting strangely in the moments before an earthquake.** Other reports describe bees abandoning their hives prior to a quake. **Some scientists believe that certain animals may be more sensitive to the vibrations that precede an earthquake.** Other scientists believe animals can sense a difference in electrical energy from Earth as it releases a gas during an earthquake.

Instant Genius
Seismologists are scientists that study earthquakes and volcanic eruptions.

174

What makes up the crust of

84

Europa, one of Jupiter's moons?

a. rock **b.** gas **c.** ice

175

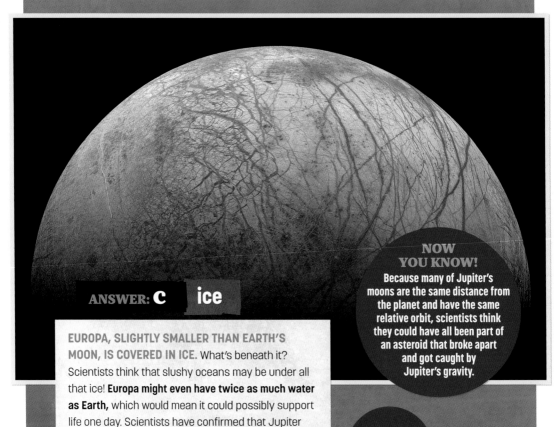

ANSWER: C ice

EUROPA, SLIGHTLY SMALLER THAN EARTH'S MOON, IS COVERED IN ICE. What's beneath it? Scientists think that slushy oceans may be under all that ice! **Europa might even have twice as much water as Earth,** which would mean it could possibly support life one day. Scientists have confirmed that Jupiter has a total of 79 moons. **Europa is one of Jupiter's four largest moons.** Together with Io, Ganymede, and Callisto, it belongs to a group of moons that scientists call the Galilean satellites. **These moons are so big, Galileo first observed them with an early version of the telescope in the early 1600s.**

NOW YOU KNOW!
Because many of Jupiter's moons are the same distance from the planet and have the same relative orbit, scientists think they could have all been part of an asteroid that broke apart and got caught by Jupiter's gravity.

Instant Genius
Of Jupiter's four Galilean moons, Callisto is the only one without a metallic core.

176

You blink less when reading from which surface?

#85

a. **a screen**

b. **a book**

c. **It's a tie.**

ANSWER: a

a screen

PEOPLE BLINK AN AVERAGE OF 15 TO 20 TIMES A MINUTE to keep their eyes moist and functioning properly. However, scientists found that, **when we are looking at a screen, we blink less than half as often as we normally would.** The artificial blue light emitted by electronic screens can cause eyestrain and blurred vision. **It can also affect our sleep cycle,** because blue light confuses the body's circadian rhythm—the way the body naturally keeps track of when to stay awake and when to sleep. **A good way to prevent eyestrain from the computer screen is by following the 20-20-20 rule.** Take a break from your screen every 20 minutes or so, look at something about 20 feet (6 m) away, then focus on it for 20 seconds. This allows your eyes to reset.

What is the foggiest place on Earth?

a. San Francisco, California

b. Hamilton, New Zealand

c. Grand Banks, Newfoundland, Canada

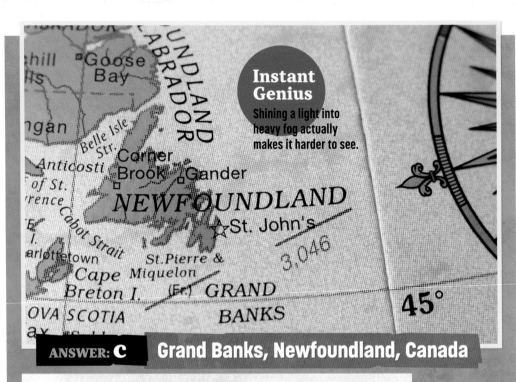

ANSWER: C **Grand Banks, Newfoundland, Canada**

FOG FORMS WHEN COOLING TEMPERATURES CAUSE WATER MOLECULES IN THE AIR TO CONDENSE AND FORM TINY WATER DROPLETS. The water droplets remain suspended in the air until warmer temperatures cause them to evaporate. **Although places along the Pacific coast such as San Francisco and New Zealand are famously foggy,** the foggiest place on Earth is found in the Grand Banks of Newfoundland, a Canadian province that has some of the thickest fog in the world, thanks to cold temperatures that interact with the warmer current of the Atlantic Ocean. **What makes the Grand Banks uniquely fog-friendly is that the entire area is located where the colder Labrador Current crosses over the warmer Gulf Stream.** This difference in current temperatures creates the perfect condition for thick blankets to form almost daily.

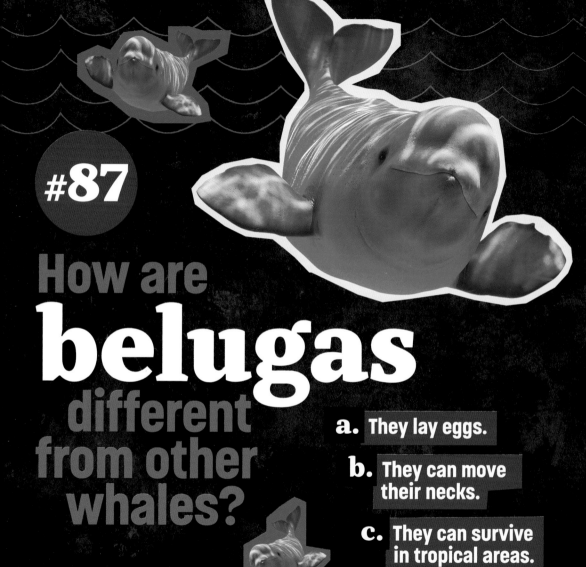

#87

How are **belugas** different from other whales?

a. They lay eggs.

b. They can move their necks.

c. They can survive in tropical areas.

They can move their necks.

WHALES, LIKE MOST OTHER MAMMALS, HAVE SEVEN BONES IN THEIR NECKS. However, most whales' neck bones are fused together, making it easier for them to keep their giant heads straight while swimming. **To turn their heads, these whales would need to turn their whole bodies.** Beluga neck bones are not fused together, however, so **belugas can turn, nod, and even shake their heads on their own!** The extra mobility also helps them hunt in shallow waters and avoid potential predators.

NOW YOU KNOW!
Beluga whales are closely related to the narwhal, sometimes called the "unicorn of the sea."

Instant Genius
Beluga whales can swim backward.

George Washington led the charge to make Thanksgiving a national holiday.

#88

EVERY FOURTH THURSDAY IN NOVEMBER, AMERICANS CELEBRATE THANKSGIVING as a day to express gratitude for the year before winter sets in. But who decided we should have an annual day of feast in the United States? **George Washington first called for a national day of thanks in 1789 to celebrate the end of the American Revolution.** Other presidents called for similar onetime celebrations. **But a writer and editor named Sarah Josepha Hale was responsible for convincing people that Thanksgiving should be a national holiday** that happens every year. She thought a holiday focused on giving thanks would help unite the country. She spent more than 30 years writing articles and sending letters to government officials to advocate for the holiday. **Finally, in 1863, President Abraham Lincoln declared Thanksgiving a national holiday.**

Instant Genius

Sarah Josepha Hale wrote "Mary Had a Little Lamb."

In what year did the first sports team visit the White House?

#89

a. 1865 b. 1901 c. 1923

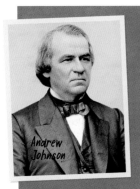
Andrew Johnson

WHEN PRESIDENT ANDREW JOHNSON INVITED TWO BASEBALL TEAMS—the Washington Nationals and the Brooklyn Atlantics—to the White House in 1865, he was making history: No sports teams had ever been invited to the White House before. **This was the beginning of what would eventually become a long-standing tradition**—gatherings between elite American athletes and the sitting president at the White House. **However, not until 1981, with Ronald Reagan's presidency, did athletes visiting the Rose Garden become a tradition.** During these gatherings, Reagan famously played catch with Washington, D.C.'s football team after they won the Super Bowl, and even allowed Harry Carson, a football player for the New York Giants, to **dump popcorn on his head in celebration of the team's Super Bowl win.**

A baseball game in 1866

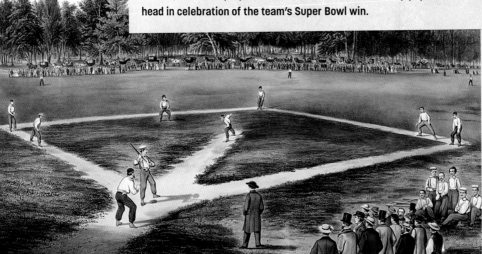

What does the word *sushi* mean in Japanese?

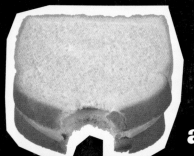

a. small bite

b. raw fish

c. sour rice

Japan's Great Kantō earthquake in 1923 might have helped make sushi popular, as sushi chefs displaced by the event moved elsewhere.

ANSWER: C

sour rice

SUSHI IS A DISH MADE FROM COLD BALLS OR ROLLS OF RICE served with raw or cooked fish, vegetables, or egg, then wrapped in seaweed and rice. **The rice is seasoned with vinegar, which gives it a slightly sour taste.** Although traditional sushi is associated with Japan, the idea might not have originated there. **The first mention of cooked rice served with salted fish appears in a fourth-century Chinese dictionary.** Using fermented rice helped preserve the fish, which meant that it could stay fresher longer. In the eighth century, the idea of sushi was probably brought to Japan. **Japanese chefs combined the fish and rice, making it a complete dish for the first time.** Only street vendors in Tokyo originally sold sushi. Later, it started popping up in restaurants all over the country. By the 1970s, sushi bars were becoming popular worldwide.

Instant Genius

Los Angeles, California, was the first U.S. city to serve sushi.

188

ANSWER: **False**

IF YOUR PET GETS SICK AFTER MUNCHING ON GRASS, YOU'RE NOT ALONE. For a long time, people thought that most cats and dogs chewed grass on purpose, to make themselves vomit if they had an upset stomach. **But studies have shown that most cats and dogs don't get sick after eating the blades of green.** One study showed that only 22 percent of dogs vomited after doing so. The same researchers conducted a similar study with cats, and they found a similar result. **Some scientists think that pets eat grass because of a nutrient deficiency in their diets.** Others suggest that dogs and cats are acting on an instinct left over from when their wild ancestors regularly ate everything or, in the case of cats, **ingested grass to clean the parasites out of their digestive systems.**

Instant Genius

The need to eat nonfood substances as a result of a nutrient deficiency is an eating disorder called pica.

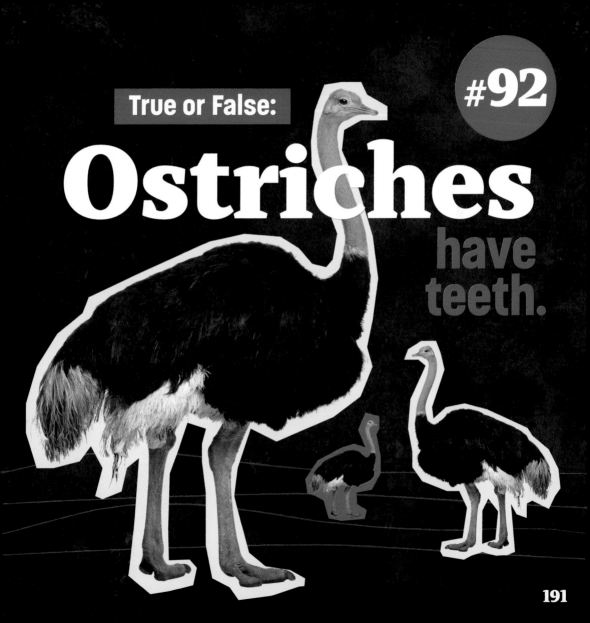

True or False:

Ostriches
have teeth.

#92

191

No dentist for me!

ANSWER: **False**

OSTRICHES, LIKE ALL LIVING BIRDS, HAVE NO TEETH. However, that wasn't always the case. Birds are related to dinosaurs, which had lots of teeth. **Fossil records from 150 million years ago show that ancient birds had teeth, too.** Over time, birds stopped growing teeth altogether, and started using their beaks instead. **Why did birds ditch their teeth?** One theory looks at how difficult it is for chicks to grow teeth while developing in their eggs. Bird ancestors spent 60 percent of the time in their eggs forming teeth. **By skipping teeth, the shorter hatching schedule shortens the time they are vulnerable and defenseless while growing inside their eggs.**

NOW YOU KNOW!
Ostriches, the tallest living birds, swallow grit—sand, shells, and tiny pebbles—to help them crush their food. Many other birds do this, too, including chickens and turkeys.

#93 What machine is most like the human heart?

a. a mini computer

b. a big pump

c. a recycling plant

193

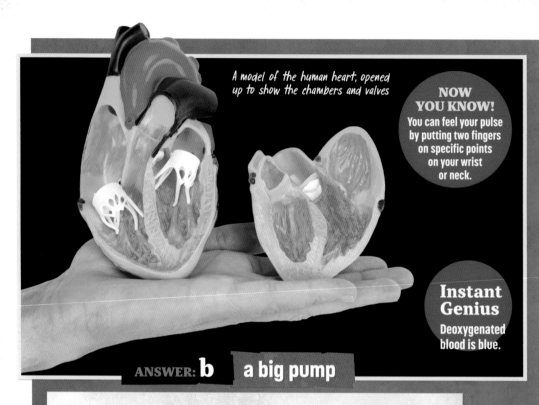

A model of the human heart, opened up to show the chambers and valves

ANSWER: b **a big pump**

THE HEART IS ONE LARGE PUMP MADE OF MUSCLE AND BLOOD VESSELS. Its job is to pump blood to the rest of your body through arteries, capillaries, and veins. **Our blood carries oxygen and nutrients to all of our organs and other tissues.** Arteries carry blood from the heart to our body tissue, veins carry the deoxygenated blood back to the heart, and capillaries exchange oxygenated and deoxygenated blood. **The heart is made up of four chambers that each have their own valve,** opening and closing to allow blood to flow out of the heart. **The beating you feel in your chest is the opening and closing of those valves.** Deoxygenated blood enters one side of the heart, is pumped to the lungs and back to be reoxygenated, **then pumped all around the body again from the other side of the heart.**

Who was the Taung child?

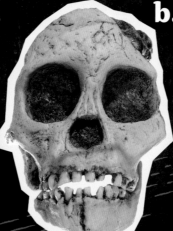

#94

a. a famous young actor

b. a skull from the first early human species discovered

c. a 10-year-old with the highest IQ ever recorded

195

a skull from the first early human species discovered

IN 1924, MINERS WORKING IN A SOUTH AFRICAN QUARRY STUMBLED UPON AN AMAZING DISCOVERY—the fossilized brain and skull of a 3-year-old child that date back 2.3 to 2.8 million years. **Discovered in Taung, South Africa, the child belonged to an early human species known as *Australopithecus africanus*.** Anthropologists later determined that the Taung child walked upright like a human on two legs, unlike other apes that usually walk with all four limbs. This was a major discovery for anthropologists, because **the Taung child was the first evidence they'd ever seen of early humans that could walk upright.** The skull was also one of the first early human fossils to ever be found in Africa, and it drew attention to a region where other early humans would later be discovered.

Instant Genius

Scientists believe the Taung child died from an eagle attack.

95

What is
El Niño?

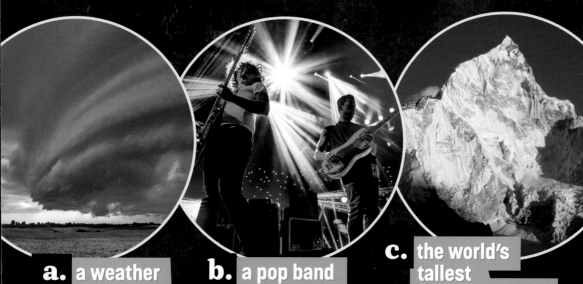

a. a weather pattern

b. a pop band

c. the world's tallest mountain peak

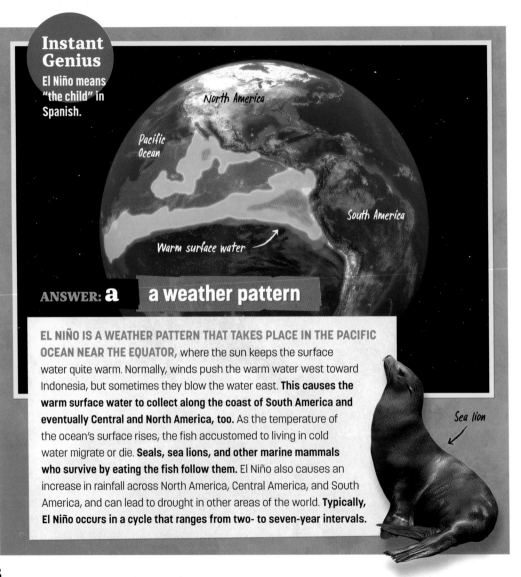

El Niño means "the child" in Spanish.

North America

Pacific Ocean

South America

Warm surface water

ANSWER: a   **a weather pattern**

EL NIÑO IS A WEATHER PATTERN THAT TAKES PLACE IN THE PACIFIC OCEAN NEAR THE EQUATOR, where the sun keeps the surface water quite warm. Normally, winds push the warm water west toward Indonesia, but sometimes they blow the water east. **This causes the warm surface water to collect along the coast of South America and eventually Central and North America, too.** As the temperature of the ocean's surface rises, the fish accustomed to living in cold water migrate or die. **Seals, sea lions, and other marine mammals who survive by eating the fish follow them.** El Niño also causes an increase in rainfall across North America, Central America, and South America, and can lead to drought in other areas of the world. **Typically, El Niño occurs in a cycle that ranges from two- to seven-year intervals.**

Sea lion

198

#96

True or False:

All planets in our solar system have **moons.**

ANSWER: **False**

IN OUR SOLAR SYSTEM, NEITHER VENUS NOR MERCURY HAS A MOON. Although scientists aren't entirely sure why, they believe that it has to do with their proximity to the sun. **Because Mercury is the closest planet to the sun, and then Venus the second closest after that, the pull of the sun may be too strong for smaller objects, like moons, to orbit around the planets.** Most of our solar system's moons likely formed from gas and dust circulating around planets, but some were wandering bodies like asteroids that form somewhere else in the solar system and were pulled inward by a planet's gravity as it passed by. **Sometimes they end up crashing into a planet, creating craters like you can see on Mercury's surface.**

Instant Genius

There are more than 200 moons in our solar system.

Mercury and Venus to scale

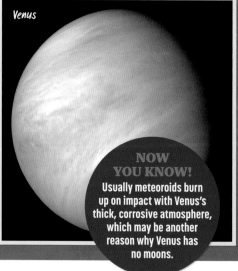

Venus

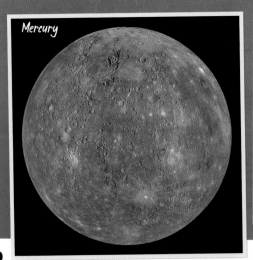

Mercury

NOW YOU KNOW!

Usually meteoroids burn up on impact with Venus's thick, corrosive atmosphere, which may be another reason why Venus has no moons.

97

In six years,
how many kittens
can descend from
a single house cat?

a. 60 **b.** 600 **c.** 66,000

ANSWER: C

66,000

UNSPAYED FEMALE CATS, KNOWN AS QUEENS, CAN GIVE BIRTH TO TWO LITTERS EVERY YEAR for most of their lives after they reach maturity. On average, two or three of these kittens grow up to have their own kittens. **Once a mother's kittens start having kittens of their own, their family tree starts to blossom rapidly.** By the third year there might be 376 cats, and by the sixth year there could be a whopping 66,088! Outdoor queens usually give birth only in the warmer months of spring and summer. **Because indoor cats don't experience the seasons in the same way, they can have babies year-round.** The size of a cat's litter can vary, depending on the breed. Siamese cats, for instance, usually have larger litters of about 10 or more kittens, and Persians have smaller litters, with sometimes only one kitten.

Instant Genius

A cat's pregnancy lasts for about two months.

Where were the world's oldest known snakes found?

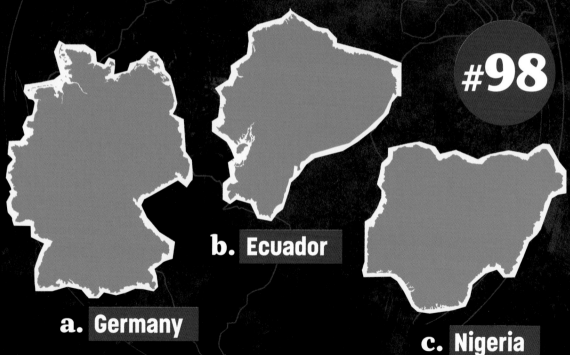

#98

b. Ecuador

a. Germany

c. Nigeria

IN 2020, A PALEONTOLOGIST IN GERMANY READ ABOUT AN UNNAMED SNAKE SPECIES and set out to learn more about it. With the help of another paleontologist, he gathered four fossilized skeletons from museum collections. The scientists discovered **these skeletons were from a new species of python estimated to be at least 47 million years old,** making them the world's oldest known snakes! The ancient pythons were more than 38 inches (97 cm) long. The fossilized pythons were a shock to scientists. Before the discovery, **many scientists thought pythons first came from areas south of the equator, where most snakes live today.**

Most animals have folds in their brains.

#99

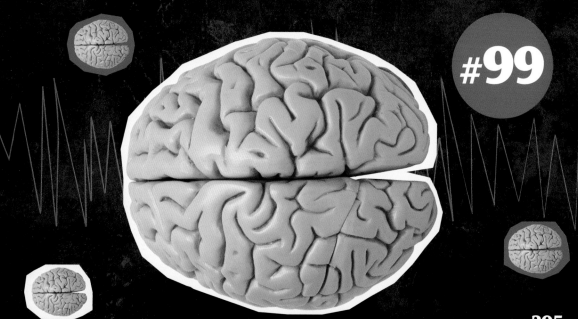

ALTHOUGH OUR BRAINS LOOK LIKE WRINKLED RAISINS, most animals' brains are actually smooth. **Humans are born with folded brains, and these folds aren't random.** All humans have the same pattern of ridges (called gyri) and grooves (called sulci). These folds add surface area to your brain, creating more space for thoughts and memories. **Generally, bigger brains have folds, and smaller brains—such as those in rats and mice—are smooth.**

Instant Genius

Rats can remember a path through a maze for up to 25 hours.

Want to time me?

The first **smartphone** was released in which year?

#100

a. 1983
b. 1992
c. 2001

THE WORLD'S FIRST PERSONAL CELL PHONE WAS INVENTED IN 1983. The original cell phone was very expensive, and nearly a foot (0.3 m) long! **It only allowed for about 30 minutes of talking time before its battery died.** Over the next decade, engineers improved upon the mobile phone, adding features and functionality. **In 1992, IBM invented the world's first smartphone, and released it to the public in 1994. This smartphone was called the Simon Personal Communicator,** and it was about the size of a brick. Still, for the first time ever, **you could talk on the phone, send emails and texts, fax documents, have a calendar, and make appointment reminders,** all from the palm of your hand—which, at the time, had never been done before!

Instant Genius

The most popular smartphone, the iPhone, was invented in 2007.

What's the largest carnivore on land?

a. tiger

b. brown bear

c. polar bear

polar bear

THOUGH THEY MIGHT LOOK CUTE AND CUDDLY, POLAR BEARS ARE ANYTHING BUT. In the Arctic, they are apex predators, which means that they are at the top of the food chain in their ecosystem. They eat seals, walruses, and whale carcasses. **Adult male polar bears can weigh anywhere from 880 to 1,320 pounds (400–600 kg)—more than two snowmobiles!** From end to end, they measure between 7 feet, 10 inches and 8 feet, 6 inches (2.4 and 2.6 m). **Each claw alone is nearly 2 inches (5 cm) long.** In addition to their large stature, they maintain their status as the heavyweight carnivore champions of the Arctic with their thick winter coats that conserve nearly all their body heat in the frigid climate, as well as a layer of fat under their skin that can be as thick as 4.5 inches (11.4 cm).

Instant Genius

Polar bears are a semiaquatic animal because they spend as much time in water as on land.

Spot the 7 Random Differences:

Turn to page 215 for the answers! **211**

Index

Page numbers in *italic* refer to images.

Photo Credits

The publishers would like to thank the following for the use of their images. While every effort has been made to credit images, the publishers will be pleased to correct any errors or omissions in future editions of the book.

t = top; b = bottom; l = left; r = right; c = center

123rf.com: pp. 10(r), 85(bl), 169.

Alamy: pp. 12(br), 18(b), 20(br), 25, 28(br), 32(t), 36(r), 64(t), 65(l,c,r), 75(c), 81(r), 126(c), 138(b), 167(br), 172, 179(r), 196(tr), 198(t), 204(t), 206(b).

Dr Neil Davies: p. 28(t).

Dreamstime: pp. 1, 2(tl,br), 4, 5(tr,c), 6(c,br), 7(tr,bl), 8–9, 10(bl), 11(cl,cr,bc), 13, 14(bl,br), 15, 16(t,bl,br), 17(l,c,r), 19(l,c,r), 21, 23, 24(tr,br), 27(cl,bl,br), 29, 30, 31, 32(br), 33, 34(t,cr), 35, 36(bl), 37, 38(br), 39(l,c,r), 40(main photo), 41, 42(l,br), 43, 44(bl,r), 45, 46(t,br), 47(cl,c,br), 48(b), 49(c,bl,br), 50(r), 51, 52(tr,br), 53, 54(t,b), 55(cl,bl,br), 56(t), 57, 58(t,b), 59(tr,cr,bc), 60(t,br), 61, 62, 63(cl,cr,bc), 64(br), 67, 68, 69(l,c,r), 70(tl,br), 71, 72, 73, 75(cl), 77, 79(t,cr), 79, 80(br), 81(l,c), 82(tl,r), 83, 84(background), 85(bl,br), 86, 87, 88(tr,br), 90, 91(cl,cr,bc), 92(t,br), 93, 94(br), 95, 96(br), 97(tr,cr,bc), 98(t,br), 99, 100(tl,cr), 101, 102(t,cr), 104(tr), 105, 106(t,br), 107(l,c,r), 109, 110(br), 113, 114, 115(l,cr,br), 116(tr,-bl,br), 117, 118(tl,bl), 119, 120(main photo,tr), 121, 122(r), 123(bl), 125, 126(tl,bl), 127, 129, 131(cr,br), 132(br), 133, 134(t), 135, 136(tcr,main photo), 137, 139, 140(t,bc), 143, 145(cr,bl,br), 146(t,cr), 149, 151, 152(l,bc), 153, 154(tl,t,br), 156(t,br), 157, 159, 160(t), 161, 162, 163(l,c,r), 164(t,br), 165(tr,bl,br), 166(main image,br), 167(bl,c), 168(t), 179(bl,r), 174(t), 175(l,c,r), 177, 178(t,cl), 179(l,c), 180, 181, 182(bl,r), 183, 184(bl), 185, 186(tr), 187(cl,bl,br), 188(tl,t), 189, 190, 191, 192, 193(cl,cr,bl), 194, 195(l,c,br), 196(bc), 197(l,c,r), 198(bl), 199, 201, 202, 203(l,c,r), 204(br), 205, 206(tr), 207, 208(bl), 209(l,c,r), 210(b), 211(t,b), 215.

Carsten Egevang (The Greenland Institute of Natural Resources/The Artic Tern Migration Project): p. 56(cr,br).

Getty Images: pp. 12(t), 20(tr), 22(br), 50(bc), 66, 96(t), 128(br).

iStockphoto: pp. 40(br), 80(t), 89, 132(t), 147, 148, 155.

Library of Congress: p. 186(tl).

NASA (National Aeronautics and Space Administration): pp. 26(t), 74(main photo,tr), 111, 134(br), 144(t,cr), 150(r), 176, 200(bl,br).

Nature Picture Library: pp. 22(tl), 85(c), 123(c,br), 130, 210(cl).

Science Photo Library: pp. 18(tl), 138(tr), 172.

Smithsonian Institution (Collection of the Smithsonian National Museum of African American History and Culture, Gift of A'Lelia Bundles/Madam Walker Family Archives): p. 168(l).

Shinji Sugiura: p. 38(tl,tr) – Sugiura, S. (2020) Active escape of prey from predator vent via the digestive tract. Current Biology 30: R867–R867 (https://doi.org/10.1016/j.cub.2020.06.026).

Wellcome Collection: p. 48(tr).

Wikimedia Commons: pp. 26(br), 75(br), 76(main photo,bc), 94(tc,tr), 103, 104(b), 108(tr,bc), 110(main photo), 112(t,cr), 122(tl), 124, 128(tr), 131(tr), 141, 142, 150(bc), 158, 160(cr), 168(bc), 171, 174(cr), 184(tr,bc), 186(b), 200(cr), 208(r).

Credits

Library of Congress Cataloging-in-Publication Data is available
upon request.

ISBN 978-0-593-51643-0 (trade)
ISBN 978-0-593-51644-7 (lib. bdg.)
ISBN 978-0-593-51645-4 (ebook)

COVER PHOTO CREDITS:
Front Cover Photo: Shutterstock.
Back Cover Photo: Dreamstime.

MANUFACTURED IN ITALY
10 9 8 7 6 5 4 3 2 1
First Edition

The publisher would like to thank the following people for their
contributions to this book: Melina Gerosa Bellows, President,
Fun Factory Press, and Series Creator and Author; Priyanka
Lamichhane, Editor and Project Manager; Chad Tomlinson,
Art Director; Heather McElwain, Copy Editor; Mary Stephanos,
Fact-checker; Potomac Global Media: Kevin Mulroy, Publisher;
Barbara Brownell Grogan, Editor in Chief; Thomas Keenes,
Designer; Susannah Jayes and Ellen Dupont, Picture Researchers;
Jane Sunderland and Heather McElwain, Contributing Editors

BRIGHT
MATTER
BOOKS